About the author

Noa Belling has a passion for sharing practical wisdom from her profession as a psychotherapist with a specialisation in the mind–body relationship and holds a Masters degree in somatic (mind–body) psychology through Naropa University. She has many years of experience working as a psychotherapist in private practice and as an executive coach and facilitator of workshops in the corporate sector. Noa also teaches psychology students and fellow mental health professionals how to incorporate body-based skills in their practice and presents talks to a wide range of audiences on topics such as stress management, leadership and team development, wellness and mindfulness.

Noa is an internationally published, bestselling and award-winning author. Her journey as an author began in 2001 with *The Yoga Handbook*, which went on to become an international bestseller and was translated into many languages. This was followed by other yoga titles and, more recently, with *The Mindful Body* (2018) and *The Happiness Workout* (2020).

To learn more about Noa's work, visit noabelling.com

Noa Belling

stress
stress
stress
stress
LESS

Managing anxiety in a modern world

ROCKPOOL

A Rockpool book
PO Box 252
Summer Hill
NSW 2130
Australia

rockpoolpublishing.com
Follow us! f ⓘ rockpoolpublishing
Tag your images with #rockpoolpublishing

Published in 2023, by Rockpool Publishing

ISBN: 9781922785633

Design and typsetting by Daniel Poole, Rockpool Publishing
Edited by Jess Cox

 A catalogue record for this book is available from the National Library of Australia

Printed and bound in China
10 9 8 7 6 5 4 3 2 1

Disclaimer

This book is designed to provide helpful information on the subjects discussed. It is not intended as a substitute for medical advice or treatment. Care has been taken to deliver information and advice in a measured way, with consideration of what is beyond the scope of the advice of this book, such as that it is not recommended as the sole treatment method for those diagnosed with a psychological disorder as defined by the current edition of the *Diagnostic and Statistical Manual of Mental Disorders*. For diagnosis and treatment of any medical or psychological condition, it is recommended to consult with a medical or mental health professional. The publisher and author are not responsible for any specific health needs that may require medical supervision, and are not liable for any damages or negative consequences from any treatment, action or application to any person reading or following the information in this book. Regarding the physical exercise practices, care has been taken to introduce practices with consideration of varying physical abilities. The author and publisher advise readers to take full responsibility for their safety and to know and adhere to their limits.

'Peace isn't an
experience free
of challenges,
free of rough and
smooth, it's an
experience that's
expansive enough
to include all that
arises without feeling
threatened.'

— **Pema Chödrön**

Contents

Complete list of exercises

Foreword

Stress has become so prevalent in life these days that we hardly know when we are experiencing it. In response, Noa has written a most valuable resource. It is a practical, down-to-earth guide that assists us to recognise how stress is manifesting in our lives and then offers practical steps for living a life less driven by stress. It is a book that will help us regain and maintain our health and sense of well-being while supporting our opening to the simple joys of being alive. This can ripple outwards through our actions and words to inspire others – our families, friends, colleagues and communities – to flourish too.

I first met Noa in 2000, when she entered the Graduate Somatic Psychology Program at Naropa University. She was an excellent student, an enthusiastic learner committed to using her knowledge to help others live healthier and more satisfying lives. This wonderful book is a testament to the depth and integration of her continued professional development and her capacity as an author. Noa has the ability to take complex scientific information, synthesise it and present it in a way that makes it easily accessible to anyone. Chapter 2 is an essential cornerstone offering a simple guide to understanding the specifics of how stress manifests in the body and mind so that we can catch it early. From there, the book is filled with a wide variety of accessible practices to choose from depending on personal preference and homes in on the two most common mental health challenges of our time: anxiety and depression. Each practice has the ability to restore balance, refresh energy and refocus our minds on what really matters.

Truly a gem, this is a book I will return to again and again. Bravo Noa, and thank you for this beautiful gift to the world.

Zoe Avstreih, LP, CAT, BC–DMT
Professor Emeritus, Naropa University
Founder and Director of the Center for the Study of Authentic Movement
Boulder, Colorado, USA

Preface

n this book, I aim to share accessible, evidence-based skills that can help all of us promote mind–body well-being, enhance vitality and increase joy for life. Scientifically backed mind and body perspectives are integrated with timeless practical wisdom.

Stress Less came into being through the global pandemic that sent stress, anxiety and depression levels soaring throughout the world. In my many conversations with clients through this time I found two things particularly helpful. The first is a framework for understanding mental health in concrete terms, in this case relating to biological survival responses and our ready access to our relaxation response that can be deliberately cultivated for mental and physical health. The second is the knowledge that there is something that we can do about how we feel. So if we feel down or really anxious, there is a tool that we can use that can make a real difference and open us to align with our resourcefulness again. In this we get to choose time and time again to step into our empowerment and ability to make a positive difference in our lives. Then, each time we bounce back we tone our resilience muscles to help us in future. The applications for these tools are also endless, applying to our personal and internal experience as much as to our professional challenges and pursuits.

The tools do not represent a particular psychological approach. Instead, they draw on general principles for working with anxiety, depression and stress from mind and body perspectives. There are also basic elements of mindfulness woven through different chapters, such as opportunities to focus the mind in particular ways or experiment with breathing more slowly and fully. Mindfulness practices are proving especially effective and sustainable in easing symptoms of stress, anxiety and depression. This is because of their naturally calming, centring and focusing effects that can boost qualities like inner peace, joy and the ability to be solution-focused.

The tools are designed to be accessible and immediately effective, with a variety of options to choose from to suit different people. They can open a window of hope and help us breathe easier no matter what is going on in the world outside us. Applicable to personal healing and growth as well as to employee well-being and honing performance excellence, there are tools to fit many different circumstances. They can also complement consultation with a mental health professional should this be appropriate.

My wish for you is that this book transforms your relationship with stress in deeply meaningful and wonderful ways. My wish is also that this transformation flows outwards to nourish your experience of life, touch the lives of others and energise your unique contributions to our world.

Noa

Introduction

'Stress is the health epidemic of the 21st century.' — **World Health Organization**

 tress is part of life. In the right doses, it is helpful and motivating for our learning, growth and the achievement of our goals. But, at times, navigating life's ups and downs and unpredictability can be more stressful than we can bear. We might chronically push ourselves or feel pushed beyond our limits when juggling family, social and work commitments, or we might receive difficult news or feel weighed down by a big decision we need to make.

Stress is our body's reaction to threat, pressure, pain or strain of any kind. In stressful moments, our heart rate may speed up; our breathing can become erratic; physical tension may mount; and worry, anxiety or overwhelm can cloud our judgment. If stress is prolonged or intense, we might sink into resignation, lethargy, depression or helplessness. We may get so used to being in a state of chronic stress, we barely notice that we're stressed at all, feeling like this is just how life is. For some people, stress can even be seen as a sign of success or something to laugh about in ourselves and each other, rather than something to take responsibility for. But no matter if we deny, ignore, minimise or glorify our stress, it tends to catch up with us, usually with some kind of crisis.

Our bodies are designed to react quickly to stress and then, following threatening moments, return to feeling safe, calm and centred again. But this return to calm does not always happen, especially when we accumulate many big and small stresses over time, or when we keep stress alive in our thoughts and imaginations. Then our stress responses can become chronic, even though they may settle into the background of our awareness. Anxiety and depression are the two most common forms of chronic stress. Anxiety can leave us feeling wired, irritable and distracted. Depression can leave us feeling depleted, tired and unmotivated.

Over time, chronic stress can be detrimental to our health and well-being. Chronic stress can interfere with immune system functioning as well as digestion and quality of sleep. It can cause headaches and physical pains, deplete our energy and lead us to self-sabotaging behaviours such as eating badly, not exercising or over-indulging. It is a state in which our bodies, all the way down to our cells, become primed for defence, protection and fixation on danger.

With chronic or frequent stress, we can still have times of feeling uplifted woven through our days but feeling truly relaxed, centred and joyful can be elusive.

Cell danger response

We know how stress penetrates deep into our cells thanks to the work of Dr Robert Naviaux, who discovered what he calls a 'cell danger response'. He found that the mitochondria inside our cells perform two roles. One role is energy production to fuel our lives, and the other is sensing and responding to safety or danger in our internal or external environment. When we feel relaxed and safe, the mitochondria are in energy-production mode. But when we sense danger, and even when we feel stressed for no apparent reason, the 'cell danger response' is triggered, with our cells switching off energy production as mitochondria move into defence and protection mode.

This helps us understand how deeply stress can affect our energy levels. Health is also optimised when our cells are in energy-production mode. They can freely carry out their functions, such as taking in nutrients from food, converting those nutrients into energy, fighting off pathogens and carrying out a range of specialised functions in support of our body's health, growth and restoration.

What triggers stress

Stress, anxiety and depression have become signs of our times. We have lived through a global pandemic with fears that more may follow. We continue to face global crises such as climate change and war, or threats of war, in parts of the world that affect us all. Then there is our modern, fast-paced, highly competitive lifestyle, which can affect young and old alike. These are examples of collective stress triggers. Collective stress often also leaves a mental health crisis in its wake, because high levels of anxiety and fatigue can spike from stress exertion.

On a more personal level, stress can be triggered by events in our external environment, such as when something catches us by surprise or someone threatens us. It can be triggered by changing events inside our body (such as aches or pain), emotions (such as sadness or anger) and thoughts (such as self-criticism or worry). It can be triggered by our inability to process our experiences, such as relationship or work challenges. Positive changes can also be a source of stress, like when we move into a new and better home, win a promotion at work, take on a challenge that stretches our abilities, or plan to go on holiday. Stress is a fact of life. But how we respond to stress is where there is room to grow.

A helpful first step is to embrace the fact that stress is part of life. The more we can learn to be aware of stress and resourceful in response to it, the less time and energy we need waste waging battles against it. The result can be more energy, courage and motivation to address what we need to and invest in the beauty of life.

Stress Less

The toolkit provided in this book will help you face stress with greater confidence. The different tools on offer mean there is something in the book for everyone. Explore these tools in your own time and, as you go along, you can discover what works best for you and personalise your toolkit. To keep track of what works well for you, it can be helpful to keep a journal or flag the pages with your favourite exercises for future use.

This toolkit will help you:

- Recognise when you are in a stress response so you can be quicker to do something about it.
- Explore different ways to unwind from stress, anxiety and depression.
- Build stress resilience regarding different aspects of our human experience:
  - **Body and breathing** Releasing tension, replenishing energy, grounding and centring in yourself, and fine-tuning your relaxation response.
  - **Mind** Addressing negative self-talk; cultivating presence; opening your mind to hopes, dreams, inner guidance and inspiration; and stepping into conscious choice.
  - **Spirit and a sense of something greater** Connecting with nature or drawing on whatever gives you meaning and direction from personal, professional and spiritual points of view. This is woven through the book as visualisation practices you can personalise, explorations in mindfulness and simple suggestions such as standing or sitting tall to align with your wiser self and values. Note that all tools are offered in a generic way, drawing on universal, non-denominational principles.

Guide to using this book

This book is designed to be versatile. You are welcome to read it from start to finish, or dip into chapters and exercises that feel most relevant to you. There is much to be gained by reading along and just skimming through the exercises. Then you can flag what you would like to focus on more intently, and go on to discover your favourite practices. You can also return to this book in years to come and gain new insights.

At the start of the book is a list of all the exercises from all the toolkits in this book. The exercises are for anyone who experiences stress – no prior experience is necessary. You can simply start where you are. Many exercises are designed to be brief and easy to incorporate into short breaks in your day. There are also longer practices for when you have more time, with potentially transformational and lasting effects.

Book overview

First, we will cover the general landscape of human stress responses in chapters 1–2. You will have an opportunity to become clearer about your go-to stress style and find suggestions to restore balance. Then specific toolkits are introduced to address the two most common forms of chronic stress: anxiety in chapters 3–6 and depression in chapters 7–11. The toolkits cover three fundamental aspects of our human experience, which can either keep stress in place or untie it from the inside out: mind, body and breathing. You are welcome to focus on the toolkit that resonates with you most at any particular time. You can embark on this journey in your own time and dip into different toolkits as you feel ready to experience something new.

Chapters 12–15 contain a shared toolkit for anxiety and depression, offering valuable life skills that can bolster stress resilience and consolidate your progress. The toolkit includes a range of visualisation practices in Chapter 12, a meditative mindfulness practice in Chapter 13 and a mindful movement sequence in Chapter 14. If you have experience with visualisation and mindfulness or an existing meditation practice, you are welcome to refer to these chapters right away. Otherwise, access the earlier toolkits for anxiety and/or depression first and move on when you feel ready. There is also a simple thinking and writing process in Chapter 15, following the acronym 'STEPS' that you can follow to proactively steer your decision-making and your life in positive directions.

Chapter 16 includes guidelines for building a lasting sense of stress mastery. Stress mastery and opening to life can be a lifelong journey of learning and growth. Knowing you have an effective stress toolkit can make all the difference. Our brains also love novelty. While you might lose interest in one practice, you can always return to find another. This can keep up a feeling of progress, knowing there is always something you can do to help yourself.

Don't wait for a crisis before getting started

These tools are designed to train your ability to change gears from stress into a calmer, clearer frame of mind, so you can live more from your luxurious relaxation response. The key is allowing yourself the time to practise when nothing much is going on, or when your stress is mild to moderate. In the midst of a crisis, we are usually not in a frame of mind to explore new skills. But if we have allowed ourselves to become familiar with these practices, then we are more likely to utilise what we have learned in crisis moments to help turn stress around. Like a skilled animal trainer, you'll become more confident in your ability to tame the wild stress animal that lives inside you.

Don't delay seeking professional help

If you have suffered some kind of trauma that continues to haunt you, or you feel that stress, anxiety or depression have been going on for too long and worn down your ability to cope, be productive, or sleep well at night, it can be helpful to work with a mental health professional. This person can help you unpack what has been going on for you. They can also guide you with life skills to bolster stress resilience and promote personal healing in a way that is tailored to suit your particular needs. You might also benefit from speaking with a trusted psychiatrist and/or medical doctor, to assess what your body might need in support of your physical and mental health. If stress is work-place related, and you feel comfortable to do so, you might benefit from speaking with the appropriate person in the work environment to consider helpful options.

There is no need to put yourself down or think yourself a failure for needing help at times. If this is the next step on your journey, then seek that help and the sooner the better. Along with these options, this book can provide you with immediately accessible strategies to support your well-being.

Part 1

Stress self-awareness and the general landscape of stress responses

chapter 1

A stress response and a relaxation response

'Working toward balance takes a lot of ingredients. We need courage, reflection, attention, action and a push-and-pull relationship between effort and relaxation.' — **Tara Stiles**

This chapter's stress toolkit:

Exercise 1.1   A sense of your relaxation response

he dance between stress and relaxation is what life is all about, propelling us into endless cycles of activity and rest. We need a balance of them both to feel alive, achieve what we would like and feel fulfilled. This chapter introduces both ends of the experiential spectrum and explains how the body's nervous system generates them. By knowing this, you can quickly catch your body launching into a stress response, do something about it, and find your way back to being calm and collected. You can also grow your relationship with your relaxation response for all the benefits to mind and body it can provide.

The body's stress response

Stress is always about feeling unsafe. It usually involves feeling threatened or challenged in some way, which might be real or imagined. On a physiological level, our bodies are instinctively gearing up to fight, flee or hide for our survival. The acute stress responses of fight or flight were first described in the 1920s by American physiologist, Walter Cannon. Since then, a range of stress responses have been identified beyond fight and flight. This chapter introduces nine different stress responses with an opportunity to identify your go-to stress style.

Survival responses like fight or flight point to the physical aspect of our stress responses, which is different from our psychological defences such as denial, projection, rationalisation and repression, identified by Sigmund Freud. When we are triggered and feeling stressed, both psychological and physical defences might show up. They are part of our hardwiring as humans. But our physical stress responses jump in first: it's like we are wired to act first, ask questions later as a matter of speed in service of survival.

The stress response we jump to is not voluntary. In the adrenalised moment, our knee-jerk reactions leap forward automatically. With self-awareness, we can grow our ability to recognise, rein in and re-route our reactions in voluntary and mindful directions. This opens up space to respond to stress differently.

A stress tipping point

We all have a tipping point of how much stress we can handle before losing our cool and flying off in survival autopilot. If we have had a lot of unresolved stress or trauma, or when we are really tired, this tipping point can come sooner, making us more frequently edgy, irritable, and perhaps moody or nervous. If we have developed stress resilience, our tipping point is pushed out – we can part the seas of stress for longer. Then we can retain a sense of being in control and resourceful, and can tolerate more stress before falling over the edge into survival mode. We also are more likely to live from a place of calmer clarity fuelled by our relaxation response.

The relaxation response

The relaxation response is our body's way of unwinding from stress and opening into calmer, clearer presence. It also enhances our ability to connect in heartfelt ways with each other. The term was popularised by Herbert Benson, a Harvard physician, in his book *The Relaxation Response* (1975). He defined the relaxation response as 'a physical state of deep rest that changes the physical and emotional responses to stress . . . and is the opposite of the fight or flight response.' Dr Benson's methods, such as abdominal breathing, repeating soothing words (such as 'peace' or 'calm'), visualising beautiful peaceful scenes, and prayer and yoga, remain relevant today and enjoy abundant scientific validation since then.

Exercise 1.1

A sense of your relaxation response

Pause for a moment. Take a long, slow breath in, yawning if you like, perhaps stretching out your body. When you are ready, let your breath out, long and slow. Take one or two more deep breaths, lengthening each exhalation, perhaps with a sigh. As you go along, draw your breath in to fill your belly then your chest. Then let go of tension as you breathe out. Settle yourself so you feel grounded through both feet; if you are sitting, sit evenly over your sitting bones too. Press down through your feet and lengthen your spine so you feel comfortably upright and calmly alert. Perhaps you can feel held between earth and sky. Aligning yourself with the natural world in this way can support mental clarity. You might also place a hand over the centre of your chest for some soothing support. How do you feel now? If you were carrying stress, has it eased somewhat? This is your relaxation response in action.

Stress and relaxation from our nervous system's point of view

Today, our understanding of the stress and relaxation responses has grown significantly. One leading theory in understanding how the nervous system is at the root of both our stress and relaxation responses is polyvagal theory, which is the work of Dr Stephen Porges. According to polyvagal theory, the autonomic nervous system functions as a finely tuned sensory system, constantly scanning for safety and danger cues within ourselves, and in our relationships and interactions with the world.

Neuroception

Dr Porges coined the term 'neuroception' to describe the unconscious, spontaneous process that sets in motion either a stress response when we sense even a hint of danger, or a relaxation response when we sense safety. From the perspective of the nervous system, we can only feel relaxed when we feel safe.

Safe? Danger? Complete overwhelm?

The autonomic nervous system regulates involuntary physiological processes such as heart and breathing rates, blood pressure, and digestion. It gives us the feeling of stress, such as our heart racing and tense muscles, or the feeling of being relaxed and breathing easy. The autonomic nervous system contains three divisions, which each govern a different aspect of our stress or relaxation responses. Two of the divisions belong to the calming parasympathetic nervous system. They operate through the vagus nerve in two distinct pathways: the ventral and dorsal vagus nerve pathways. Each triggers completely different physiological responses as detailed below.

1. Feeling safe

- Our relaxation response comes online as our calming, parasympathetic nervous system makes use of the wholesome, ascending ventral vagus nerve pathway. This is the nerve pathway of well-being, happiness and sustainable energy. It lights up our ability to feel well and connect with each other in attuned, meaningful ways. It feeds into our lungs to free up our breathing; our heart to open our capacity for heartfelt connecting; our throat to free up our ability to communicate in a clear, friendly manner; our facial muscles to let us smile and engage expressively with each other; and our brain to let us think holistically, wisely and creatively.

- Stress resilience is greatly enhanced when we feel this way, so if we do experience stress, we feel in control and resourceful. This book is filled with strategies for strengthening and toning this vagus nerve pathway.

2. Sensing danger

- The sympathetic nervous system kicks in at the first sign of danger. It bypasses the calming vagus nerve to activate our mobilising stress responses such as fight or flight. It speeds up our heart and breathing rates to energise our bodies for action. Along with this comes some muscle tension, while the release of stress biochemicals such as adrenaline and cortisol make us stronger and faster to fight off or run away from danger. To use a car analogy, our bodies 'rev up' for action to defend and protect ourselves.

○ There are also reflexive ways that our nervous system might 'rev up' spontaneously. For example, we have a righting reflex to regain our balance when we fall, a startle reflex when we get a fright, and instincts like jerking a hand away from fire or urgently slamming on the brakes while driving to avoid an accident. These are not fight or flight responses; rather, they are instinctive reflexes that grip us in the moment. We can help to release the quick energy build-up by following how our body might spontaneously want to shake off the impact, eventually taking a deep sigh of relief to restore our nervous system's balance.

3. Complete overwhelm

○ If actively defending and protecting ourselves is not effective, not possible or too exhausting, or if our situation is too overwhelming, the powerfully depressing dorsal vagus nerve pathway takes over. This is a primitive, immobilising branch of the parasympathetic nervous system. With it comes a significant slowing down of the heart rate, breathing and metabolism. It involves the body and mind shutting down or withdrawing from consciousness to help us endure extreme stress. This can range from freezing in fright and going mentally blank like a deer in the headlights, to softer and dreamier options such as going numb or slipping into a floaty altered state from pain-relieving endorphins that can be released. It is also possible to pass out and collapse to the ground.

Chronic stress

If we let stress simmer, or if stress is persistent or cannot be resolved, it can become chronic. Chronic stress can cast a shadow through our days, clouding our view of reality, our ability to be resourceful and our capacity to rebound from daily triggers. When we live with a chronic belief that we are in danger or overwhelmed, we can struggle to relax or sleep well at night.

- **Anxiety**, alternatively known as an anxious freeze response, is when chronic stress leaves us wired, unsettled and prone to reactivity. It makes use of the sympathetic nervous system, speeding up our heart and breathing rates. Instead of following through with action, however, we can feel stuck and unable to decide what to do next. It can feel like driving with one foot pressing on the accelerator and the other on the brakes.

- **Depression** is when chronic stress sinks into low energy, low motivation, withdrawal, dissociation or lethargy. It makes use of the parasympathetic, dorsal vagus nerve pathway. Unremitting stress of any kind can transform the high energy of anxiety into the collapse of depression out of exhaustion. Anger that is overused, avoided or unsuccessful can also result in us collapsing inwards and feeling hopeless and depressed.

With anxiety and depression, safety can feel very far off. But it is achievable with patience, perseverance and a willingness to try out new things, such as the options offered in this book.

chapter 2

Nine stress responses and your go-to stress style

'Don't fight stress. Embrace it. Turn it on itself. Use it to make yourself sharper and more alert. Use it to make you think and learn and get better and smarter and more effective. Use the stress to make you a better you.' — **Jocko Willink**

This chapter's stress toolkit:

Exercise 2.1 What is your go-to stress style?

Exercise 2.2 Become curious about stress

tress can show up in many ways. This chapter identifies nine different stress responses for your reflection and awareness. You are invited to read through the options to notice which might be your go-to stress style. Most of us have one or two dominant stress responses, which can vary depending on our circumstance. They can also vary in intensity, sometimes showing up strongly and other times mildly. With a fight response, for example, we could fly off the handle with anger and shout or strike out, or we could simmer with irritability and agitation. Or with a flight response, we could feel like running away, or we could sit with restlessness, fidgeting and a desire to be somewhere else. One stress response can also trigger another, such as anxiety triggering a fight response, or prolonged fight or flight leading to a collapse into exhaustion or depression.

Our habitual stress responses are influenced by our basic temperament, which we are born with, and our life experiences. They can also shape our personality and way of being in the world. Here are a few examples of how our stress responses can shape us:

- A confident, fiery person who is easily able to stand up for themselves. They fight for what they believe in, and become louder or more aggressive as pressure mounts. This reflects a well-honed fight response.

- Someone who prefers a quieter, reserved and conflict-averse life. They are unlikely to stick their necks out, opting to live in the shadows as opposed to the spotlight. They may have a tendency to anxiously freeze or withdraw under pressure.

- A person who never seems to settle down. They may tend towards avoidance behaviours when stressed, and are prone to being flighty, restless and resistant to commitment, and always seem to be chasing the next new thing or exciting adventure. This could be a seasoned flight response.

Our posture can reveal our personality too. Sir Charles Sherrington, a pioneer in the field of neurophysiology, believed that posture is the 'steady maintenance of an attitude' rather than serving a purely mechanical physical function. You might imagine the uprightness of someone with bold self-confidence and the ability to hold strong, direct eye contact. They are likely to be quite comfortable with a fight response. Compare this with the hunched-over demeanour and averted gaze of a reserved and shy person, who might engage with life nervously and prefer to withdraw or reach out for help rather than tackle challenges head-on.

There is no need to judge yourself about how stress might leap forward in you and perhaps shape aspects of your personality. Our knee-jerk reactions can be out of our control. The intention in this chapter is to become more aware of how we react to stress. We can then be quicker at catching when a stress response is in play. We can also be quicker at reining in our knee-jerk reactions so we can choose how we wish to respond. We can thus reshape our way of being in life to align with values that inspire us.

The anxiety and depression toolkits in this book support different stress responses because they share common ground in terms of nervous system activation. If the energising sympathetic nervous system is engaged, then the anxiety toolkit can be supportive. If the depressing dorsal vagus nerve pathway of the parasympathetic nervous system is engaged, then the depression toolkit can be supportive. In the following tables, which toolkit is suitable for each stress response is indicated in the field called: 'Tips to restore balance'.

Bear in mind that each stress response energises particular qualities for survival and thriving, which can be helpful to us at different times. It is only when stress is too strong a driver of our lives that it can cause problems for us. For this reason, the potential gifts of particular responses are included at the end of each table to inspire us to steer our stress responses in positive directions. Or if we resist certain stress responses, we can realise they have potential benefits. We all have access to all stress responses, even though some will come more naturally to us than others because of our basic temperament and life experience.

Exercise 2.1

What is your go-to stress style?

As you read through the questions and tables that follow, ask yourself if you can relate to certain personality characteristics and consider which might be your go-to stress responses. Perhaps there are one or two that stand out, or some that feel familiar in certain circumstances or at different times of your life. Or you might notice that only some of the descriptions resonate with you. Even so, you should be able to get a feel for which stress responses you tend to fall back on.

The nine stress responses are:

- Fight
- Flight
- Anxious freeze
- Blank, numb or dissociated freeze
- Collapse, withdraw or fall into depression
- Cry for help
- Clinging
- Please and appease
- Tend and befriend

1. Fight

'Revved up' with sympathetic nervous system activation

Can you relate?

- Are you quick to irritability and anger, have little time for fear, and do not respect weakness in yourself and others?
- Do you easily stand up and speak up for yourself?
- Do you have a strong personality, and are easily confident, assertive, decisive and goal-driven?
- Are you comfortable with positions of authority and like being in control? Perhaps you believe that a firm hand is better than a kind and gentle one, especially when something needs to get done.
- Are you quite demanding and tend to hold others to very high standards, which they might not be able to fulfil? This could feed back into frustration or anger, and feeling like you need to do everything yourself or go it alone.

Fight

Body	Mind and emotions
○ Tension in upper body, chest, jaw, arms and hands	○ Anger
○ Increased blood flow to energise upper body	○ Rage
	○ Irritability
○ Puffing or inflating upper body to look bigger and stronger	○ Annoyance
	○ Volatility, possibly reacting at the slightest provocation
○ Movement or speech that's hard, forceful, powerful or explosive	○ If chronic: can lead to being conflictual, antagonistic, self-righteous or grandiose, fixating on problems and obsessing with finding solutions.
○ Voice deepening to be more booming	
○ Eyes locking on target and developing tunnel vision	
○ Hands itching to become fists or push away	
○ Breathing becomes faster and louder as if breathing fire	
○ If chronic, neck, jaw, shoulder, upper back tension and possibly jaw grinding	

Tips to restore balance

- ○ Anxiety toolkit can be helpful to ground and centre.
- ○ Connect with your heart as a counterbalance for strength.
- ○ Find healthy, dignified ways to express yourself.
- ○ Be selective to fight the good fights.
- ○ Set appropriate boundaries.
- ○ Keep up with physical exercise as an outlet for energy.
- ○ Allow for healthy ambition and being a good leader in your way.

Potential gifts

Boldness, strength, courage, assertiveness, ability to set boundaries and willingness to fight the good fight.

2. Flight
'Revved up' with sympathetic nervous system activation

Can you relate?

- Do you find yourself wanting to avoid, run away or escape from confrontation and sometimes from commitment?

- Do you avoid taking responsibility or following through on plans and goals; instead favouring new, exciting ideas or escapist behaviours?

- Do you tend to rush around or keep yourself really busy, even when there is no urgent need for it?

- Do you make yourself busy to avoid your feelings at times?

- Do you speak really fast when under pressure or excited?

- Does your mind race at times with anxious thoughts, which sometimes wind you up into a panic?

- Do you get bored easily, possibly with a short attention span? Perhaps you believe life is too short to sit still for too long, or you carry a sense that you would rather be somewhere else.

- Are you prone to your legs getting jittery or your hands becoming fidgety when you try to focus for a bit too long?

- Do you struggle to switch off your mind and relax when you need to, like when trying to go to sleep at night?

- When uncomfortable situations show up, do you avoid them for as long as possible instead of facing them head-on?

Flight

Body	Mind and emotions
o Restlessness, fidgeting	o Fear, anxiety and panic
o Movement and speech can be speedy and jittery with tendency to be in a rush	o Thoughts racing a mile a minute
	o Tendency to think and be a step (or many steps) ahead
o Increased blood flow and muscle mobilisation in lower body, mainly legs, to help run, jump and escape harm	o Possibly non-committal
	o Can lead to mania, workaholism and chronic running away from feelings
o Eyes shifty or darting as if scanning for danger or looking for where to escape to safety	o If chronic, it can lead to a tendency towards escapist, addictive behaviour and being non-committal or not following through on projects.
o Voice higher pitched and speaking can be a mile a minute	
o If chronic, it can lead to fidgeting, nail-biting and difficulty sitting still and concentrating	

Tips to restore balance

- o Anxiety toolkit can be helpful to ground, calm and centre.
- o Focus on a single object for a few breaths to focus the eyes and mind.
- o Burn off energy through aerobic exercise, such as running or skipping rope.
- o Imagine running away from danger and towards a place of safety for some sense of relief.
- o Keep up with exciting goals for a positive sense of moving forwards.

Potential gifts

Sense of freedom and agility, a drive to be productive, creative, inventive and to try new things.

3. Anxious freeze
'Revved up' with sympathetic nervous system activation and feeling stuck

Can you relate?

- Do you tend to freeze up in certain situations, perhaps social or performance situations, or when an argument flares up? You might find yourself either at a loss for words or starting to speak desperately and quickly as anxiety heats up inside you. You may not do well in heated arguments or high-pressure situations. When caught off guard or not feeling prepared, you might tense up and perhaps not know what to say or do.

- Do you tend to be indecisive or prone to 'analysis paralysis', which can slow you down or have you feel stuck at times?

- Are you prone to worrisome thinking, perhaps with 'what if' scenarios that plague your mind, slow down decision-making, make you risk averse and keep you awake at night with high anxiety?

- Have you ever felt frozen to the spot in fright or confusion, like a deer in the headlights? When it comes with your heart pounding in your chest and possibly your mind swirling with fearful thoughts, then it is an anxious freeze response. This is as opposed to going mentally blank, dissociating or feeling numb (which will be described next). It is possible to alternate between feeling anxious and going mentally blank or numb.

Anxious freeze (also known as anxiety)

Body	Mind and emotions
o Tense or rigid	o Anxiety
o Possibly shaky and trembly	o Can escalate into panic
o Could feel hot and sweaty	o Hyper-vigilance
o Breathing shallow, usually restricted to upper chest or holding your breath	o Overthinking, over-analysing or catastrophising
o Speech could be fast to match swirling or racing thoughts.	o Indecisive or confused
	o Feeling stuck
	o Feeling unsettled and unsafe
	o Self-doubt, low self-esteem due to loud inner critic

Tips to restore balance

- o Anxiety toolkit can help to ground, calm, centre and channel energy in a helpful direction.
- o Allow the body to shake and shudder off tension, and use physical exercise to release tension.
- o Bring awareness into the here and now, and grow your ability to hold it there.
- o Connect with your truth.
- o Take action – anxiety can dissolve when we are on the move.

Potential gifts

Healthy thoughtfulness to feed into mindful and considered action

4. Blank, numb or dissociated freeze

'Shut down' with parasympathetic, dorsal vagus nerve activation

Can you relate?

- Do you tend to freeze up and feel at a loss for words in heated or high-pressure situations? It might also happen when you don't feel prepared. You might tense up or automatically hold yourself still because you do not know what to say or do.

- Have you ever felt frozen to the spot in fright like a deer in the headlights? Perhaps certain situations are triggering, such as social or performance situations, or memories of a traumatic event. When the heart and mind are racing, it is an anxious freeze response. But when we go mentally blank, are at a loss for words, dissociate or go numb to what is happening, it is a numb, blank freeze response. It can feel like your body is in the room but you are not really there. While feeling frozen to the spot, you can also alternate between moments of high anxiety with a racing heart and mind, and going blank or numb.

- Under stress or in life in general, are you prone to feeling stuck, helpless or slow to figure out what is going on and what to do next?

Blank, numb or dissociated freeze

Body	Mind and emotions
○ Stillness, rigidity, coldness and numbness, possibly with a sinking feeling in the gut ○ Blank stare in the eyes ○ Verbally frozen or mute ○ Holding your breath or barely breathing	○ Non-emotional, numb ○ Going quiet ○ Dissociated, withdrawn ○ Feeling empty or lost inside or directionless ○ Feeling stuck ○ Mentally blank or foggy ○ Can be dreamy, surreal, spaced out ○ Feeling lifeless ○ Possibility of 'out of body' experience ○ Limited ability to vision or plan for the future due to feeling stuck in the past or in 'la-la land'

Tips to restore balance

○ Depression toolkit can help to motivate, inspire and gradually energise you.
○ Take a few gentle breaths, filling belly and chest to breathe new life into your nervous system.
○ Notice your surroundings to orient to the here and now.
○ Energise your body and mind through gentle exercise such as walking, Yoga and Qigong
○ Spend time in nature.
○ If chronic, seek support for unresolved shock or trauma.

Potential gifts

Opportunity to regroup and refocus, possibly leading to a perspective shift, which might be important at the time. Sensory break from reality to increase endurance through hard times.

5. Collapse, withdraw or sink into depression

'Shut down' with parasympathetic, dorsal vagus nerve activation

Can you relate?

- Do you tend to give up easily or perhaps shy away from conflict?

- Do you struggle to speak up for yourself?

- Are you prone to slipping into feeling helpless, hopeless or depressed? Perhaps you also frequently feel really alone (even when in the company of others) and melancholic?

- Do you feel easily intimidated by people who appear more confident or assertive than you?

- In heated situations, does your energy quickly drain out of you, leaving you feeling tired and helpless? Or in heated situations, do you sometimes wish you could become invisible? This can come with a tendency to dissociate or retreat into yourself like a tortoise into its shell when tensions rise. Your own imaginary world might even feel like a blissful place to be. But if you stay for too long, it can interfere with your ability to be productive and actively engage with life.

Collapse, withdraw or sink into depression

Body	Mind and emotions
○ Lack of energy and motivation	○ Feel nothing, numb
○ Fatigue or lethargy	○ Mentally blank or with brain fog
○ Flaccid muscles	○ Unmotivated and resistant to getting going
○ Feeling heavy either with complete collapse or fainting, or partial inner collapse into feelings like depression	○ Feeling all alone
	○ Tendency to isolate
	○ Shame, worthlessness
○ Heart rate, breathing and metabolism slow down significantly	○ Helpless, hopeless
	○ Could be sadness or melancholy
○ Breathing can feel like an effort	○ Empty or lost
	○ Unable to think clearly and possible gaps in memory
	○ Limited ability to envision or plan for the future
	○ If chronic, could be depressed, resigned, or achievement or social phobic.

Tips to restore balance

○ The depression toolkit can be helpful to inspire and gradually energise you

○ Come to your senses through noticing your environment, using gentle movement like stretching, moving to music or taking an easy walk.

○ Move towards the support of others or any warmth and love around you.

○ Seek support to uncover and work with the root cause of feelings and address challenges.

○ Do some soul-searching to connect with meaning and purpose, find the courage to live more fully, and take baby steps in inspiring directions.

Potential gifts

Being humble and respectful of your limits. Depression can be an opportunity to connect in deeply with yourself, do some soul-searching, reprioritise and possibly gain a sense that there is more to life than meets the eye.

Stress responses with a relational flavour:

6. Cry for help

'Revved up' with sympathetic nervous system

This is one of the first stress responses we use as babies. It is how babies let their caregivers know they need something urgently. If we are supported consistently and well enough, we learn that our needs can be met by others and become comfortable with reaching out to others for support. If support is inconsistent, we can grow a fear of abandonment that we might carry for life, or perhaps feel we need to be louder and more insistent to get our needs met. Or if we are neglected or not sufficiently met on an emotional level, we can learn emotional self-sufficiency and feel uneasy with reaching out to others for help.

Can you relate?

- Do you find it easy to express your emotions, and ask or reach out for help?

- Do you regularly seek out comfort, reassurance or validation from others? This might mean that you keep a circle of loved ones close by, speaking to them regularly, perhaps to make sure they are there for you.

- Do you believe that you deserve support from others and get angry when significant people are not there for you? Maybe you have an intense fear of abandonment that can be triggered when you think loved ones are letting you down.

- Do you rely strongly on others while feeling deficient in your own ability to self-soothe or take care of yourself?

- Have you ever felt ashamed of your intense need for the soothing and comfort of others, or self-critical of your inability to self-soothe?

Cry for help

Body	Mind and emotions
○ Reaching out for help that could be expressed through arms, eyes or voice ○ Increased blood flow to energise the upper body to reach out for support ○ Teariness (which stimulates the calming, soothing parasympathetic nervous system for some emotional soothing)	○ Anxiety ○ Desperation, despair ○ Feeling helpless ○ Separation anxiety ○ Possibly sense of helplessness ○ Neediness or possibly acting out for attention ○ Easily triggered into feeling abandoned ○ When chronic, could lead to anxious reliance on others, fear of being alone and not trusting in ability to take care of oneself

Tips to restore balance

○ The anxiety toolkit can be helpful to ground, calm and centre before channelling energy in a helpful direction.

○ Ground through the feet and feel your ability to stand on your own two feet, literally and metaphorically

○ Find opportunities to practise relying on yourself so you know that you can. Then reaching out to others can be from a healthier desire to connect rather than desperation.

Potential gifts

Being able to reach out for help when we need to and practise reciprocity. This nurtures supportive, heartfelt relationships, and possibly inspires this in others.

7. Clinging
'Revved up' with sympathetic nervous system activation

Can you relate?

- Do you struggle with standing on your own two feet to meet life's challenges, keeping key people very close by so they can do this for you, perhaps a bit more than you would like?

- Do you experience strong separation anxiety or do you need constant reassurance that significant people are not losing interest in you?

- Do you need to hold on tightly to that which is dear for fear of losing it? Maybe you've found yourself incessantly texting, calling or compulsively monitoring social media to see what a significant person is up to.

- Have you ever been told that a loved one feels stifled by your need for more closeness and constant reassurance than they are comfortable to give?

- Deep down, are you terrified of being abandoned, which can drive this clinging, mistrustful behaviour?

Clinging

Body	Mind and emotions
○ Grasping quality	○ Anxiety, panic
○ Holding on tightly or pulling into centre (may cling to a person or special object)	○ Helplessness
	○ Fear of independence
○ Resisting separation	○ Worry and fear of being alone, which can become chronic
	○ Intense fear of abandonment
	○ Constant need to connect, text, follow on social media and stay in touch
	○ Needs a lot of reassurance
	○ Uses flattery and persistent attentiveness to win favour with others
	○ Belief that 'If I let go, I will not be okay.'
	○ Mistrust of others, which can turn into controlling behaviour to get needs met

Tips to restore balance

○ The anxiety toolkit can be helpful to ground, calm and centre before channelling energy in a helpful direction.

○ Ground through your feet and place a hand over your heart for emotional soothing and to centre yourself.

○ Know that clinginess does not need to define you.

○ Find ways to grow your sense of self so you can discover the gifts of self-reliance, such as tapping into your likes and dislikes, and taking risks in trusting others not to abandon you.

○ It is okay to need reassurance from others; it is also important to be able to trust yourself and others.

Potential gifts

Holding near what is dear to us and proactively nurturing those relationships, which could be with important people and causes that touch our hearts.

8. Please and appease (also known as fawn)
'Revved up' with sympathetic nervous system activation

Can you relate?

- Do you tend to put the needs of others before your own, especially in heated situations?

- Do you suffer from frequent self-doubt?

- Do you feel that when you are with others, you easily lose touch with your truth and ability to speak up for what you believe in? Perhaps fitting in is easier for you than standing out.

- Do you struggle to say 'no' in case it causes conflict? At times, you might say 'yes' when you don't really mean it. This might come from a place of needing to keep the peace, no matter the cost to you and no matter how uncomfortable you might feel inside while going about it.

- Does it stress you out when you think people don't like you? Do you tend to want everyone to like you and not wish to cause any trouble?

Please and appease (also known as fawn)

Body	Mind and emotions
<ul><li>Active efforts to remedy the needs of others, such as fetching, carrying, or using words to appease</li><li>Making oneself small by physically contracting inwards or could lead to a feeling of squirming or tension in one's core</li><li>Tightness in the throat when needing to speak up for oneself or find what to say that might keep the peace or end conflict</li></ul>	<ul><li>Anxiety in confrontational situations and putting the needs of others first</li><li>Fear of assertiveness</li><li>Very forgiving of others (but not of oneself)</li><li>Minimising, ignoring or denying own needs and feelings</li><li>'Walking on eggshells' or anxiously trying to pre-empt, guess and serve the needs of others especially when situations become heated</li><li>Conflict averse</li><li>Prioritising being liked and nice over being real</li><li>Submissive in an active way by trying to appease others and restore peace.</li></ul>

Tips to restore balance

- The anxiety toolkit can be helpful to ground, calm and centre before channelling energy in a chosen direction
- Cultivate authenticity by becoming curious about and investing in your own interests and enjoyments
- When you are squirming inside stand on both feet to centre in yourself and find your ground. You can also place a hand over the centre of your chest and take a few soothing breaths
- Focus on self-care and finding your voice and truth to balance tendency to over-give or compulsively appease.

Potential gifts

Being helpful, adaptable and generous, possibly inspiring others to do the same. Natural skills for diplomacy and peacekeeping that can be applied to meaningful causes.

9. Tend and befriend

'Revved up' with sympathetic nervous system activation or led by wholesome, ventral vagal pathway of parasympathetic nervous system

Can you relate?

- Do you consider yourself a natural caretaker of others? Perhaps you've enjoyed taking care of those around you from a young age.
- Are you a confidante to many, and enjoy or feel driven to bring people together and take care of them, especially in times of crisis?
- Do you have a keen awareness of community and society and their effects on individuals? Do you take it upon yourself to be part of the solution and perhaps have a strong sense of duty?
- Do you feel lost or without purpose when you aren't contributing to a meaningful cause?

Tend and befriend

Body

- Strong and active protective instinct directed to circle of care
- Like the fight response, it mobilises action and energises the upper body and voice, although it has a different feel. It has a more dignified, heartfelt strength than a fight response.
- If overused, it can lead to exhaustion, compassion fatigue or burn-out.

Mind and emotions

- Heartfelt caring, compassion and empathy for others
- Strong sense of duty
- Strength of character that fuels the ability to stand up for others
- Benevolence
- If overused, it can lead to denial of one's own needs and limits or martyrdom

Tips to restore balance

- The anxiety toolkit can be helpful to ground, calm and centre before channelling energy in a helpful direction.
- Place a hand over your heart and take a few quiet, deep breaths to return awareness to yourself and your needs in the moment.
- Taking care of others and building community are noble qualities. But if anxiety drives this stress response, it can lead to overextending ourselves and burn-out. As a healthy drive, we also take care of ourselves and maintain healthy work–life balance.

Potential gifts

Passionate and powerful determination to be of service.

Exercise 2.2

Become curious about stress

Next time you catch yourself feeling stressed, rather than letting stress run away with you, pause for a moment and observe your stress. Do so with curiosity and respect, because stress is essentially your instincts trying to protect you. You might greet stress to create some distance between yourself (perhaps your wiser self) and your stress, such as inwardly saying, 'I am stressed,' or 'Hello, stress.' This moment of pause can interrupt your automatic reaction and open space for conscious response. It can free your mind so it can think more clearly about what to do next. You might also notice if your body has tensed up or collapsed in some way. You can release your posture with a deep breath and a feeling of coming to your centre.

Perhaps you can work out the kind of stress response your body has launched into such as fight, flight, freeze, or please and appease.

With time and growing self-awareness, you can learn your habitual stress responses. With the help of the tools in this book, you can feel more prepared when stress shows up. For now, take this first step of turning towards stress instead of letting it run away with you, then notice what might flow from there.

Still not clear what your dominant stress response is?

Even if you cannot find clarity about what your dominant stress response might be, or perhaps all you know for sure is that you get stressed at times, the toolkits that follow can still help you. You can simply focus on the one that interests you most.

Part 2

Growing your toolkit

chapter 3

Spotlight on anxiety

'Anxiety is like a rocking chair. It gives you something to do, but it doesn't get you very far.' — **Jodi Picoult**

This chapter's stress toolkit:

Exercise 3.1   Following a trail of possible triggers for anxiety

nxiety is the most common mental health challenge of our times. It is characterised by incessant worry, over-estimation of danger, under-estimation of our ability to cope and avoidance of triggering situations. Coming in a close second is depression, which is characterised by feelings of helplessness and worthlessness. Depression and anxiety can also co-exist or alternate.

According to the World Health Organization (WHO), 1 in 13 people globally had anxiety in 2021. But if you ask people, especially those who live in big cities where the pace is fast and the competition and pressures are high, you might find that everyone has experienced bouts of anxiety at one time or another. Some of us might even admit that anxiety is always with us, sometimes receding into the background of our awareness, at other times jumping to the fore.

Anxiety is a natural physiological response to uncertainty or fear. It is biologically designed to sharpen our senses and prepare us to take appropriate action. It can be gearing up towards fight, flight or another active stress response should it be needed. Or it can represent the pent-up energy following an active stress response, where the energy does not fully dissipate and remains in a kind of a holding pattern in the body to keep us vigilant and on edge.

At the root of anxiety is fear. Fear can express itself in many ways, such as fear of bad consequences or harm, fear of embarrassment, fear of losing control, fear of change, fear of getting ill, or fear of being rejected. If we dig a little deeper, we might also find an existential life-or-death fear. Sometimes this emerges from irrational snowball thinking, such as starting with a fear of some change that quickly becomes a fear of losing everything with thoughts of landing up destitute and unable to sustain our own lives or those of our dependants.

Fear can also show up as free-floating anxiety, unrelated to a particular trigger in the moment, which rises to the surface seemingly at random as we move through our days. This can be a sign of accumulated fear that we carry with us from past experience until we find a way to resolve or release it. Whether our fear is deeply personal or shared (such as with collective threats like pandemics, war and climate change), the bottom line is, we humans tend to be really scared!

Symptoms of anxiety

Some symptoms of anxiety include excessive worry about what might happen, a tendency to catastrophise, dwelling on the past, having difficulty concentrating or falling asleep at night due to a busy mind. This distracts us from what is happening in the present and limits our ability to tap into intelligent, creative and compassionate thinking. On a physical level, it can show up in different ways, such as tension, restlessness, fidgeting, nail-biting, headaches, digestive issues, trembling, feeling on edge or struggling to relax.

We do not need to live in fear. Remember that anxiety is a kind of freeze response, so the minute we act to confront our fears directly, test the validity of our thoughts and theories, or simply go for a walk to clear our minds, our anxiety can dissipate. New clarity and resourcefulness can then take its place. This is why anxiety can subside when we exercise. But the physical exertion of exercise only provides temporary relief if we do not address the underlying triggers or root causes for our anxiety.

The anxiety toolkit that follows can support you in several ways, drawing on modern and ancient strategies to unwind from anxiety, from mind-based interventions for slowing down or re-routing anxious trains of thought, to body- and breathing-based methods. These methods can hack into the nervous system, which creates your experience of anxiety, uprooting it at the source.

Exercise 3.1

Following a trail of possible triggers for anxiety

When next you feel anxious, pause to think: what is on your mind that might be triggering you? You might uncover a recent trigger. On deeper reflection, you might realise that more triggers lie behind it, adding to your stress levels. Sometimes there is one clear trigger, and sometimes an accumulation of triggers over days or weeks can be pressing on you. These could be linked with adversity of some kind, or with social dynamics. Or it could be due to something good in your life, such as stepping into a new role at work, that feels anxiety-provoking.

This kind of questioning can guide you to something you need to address. It could also point to the courage you need to muster to take some action or speak your truth, which can be anxiety-provoking. Thinking through these possible triggers or, if you can, talking about them with someone who cares, can slow down and organise your thinking. You can then replace unconscious mental swirling with conscious choice, helping you feel more in control as you decide what to do next.

Sometimes anxiety suddenly shows up, such as first thing in the morning and without a clear trigger. Morning anxiety can be a sign of habitual thinking coming online. Pay attention to the quiet of your mind just before that point, as you emerge from your dreams or deep sleep. Where does your mind go in the silence? When you wake up and anxiety does set in, you can go on to ask yourself, perhaps more generally, what you are afraid of at that time. This might include remnants of fear from days before. Or it might show you to a feeling from your dreams, that also could reflect some unresolved emotional issues from your past.

When anxiety becomes an anxiety disorder

Some people experience anxiety more intensely and frequently than others; this may lead to an anxiety disorder being diagnosed. There is usually not one single reason – it could grow out of various risk factors, such as genetics, epigenetics (which is the inheritance of a propensity for anxiety from our ancestors), brain chemistry, personality and adverse life events. With an anxiety disorder, anxiety interferes significantly with daily functioning and does so on most days for a period of 6 months or more.

Examples of anxiety disorders are panic disorder, generalised anxiety disorder, phobia-related disorders, obsessive compulsive disorder (OCD), health or illness anxiety (such as hypochondria) and post-traumatic stress disorder (PTSD). They usually require professional support. Medication is often a go-to strategy, although it is not always effective and can result in unwanted side effects. Fortunately, there are many non-pharmaceutical, psychological and physiological ways of working with anxiety. They can also complement medication when it might be necessary. Professional support can guide a personalised treatment plan, including an opportunity to reflect on and work with specific anxiety triggers.

Alongside consulting with a professional, the anxiety toolkit in this book can assist with easing and dissipating the energy of anxiety, and building anxiety resilience.

Anxiety in children and teenagers

The number of children and teenagers showing symptoms of anxiety is growing. Anxiety, or excessive worry that feels out of control, can alter behaviour and affect many aspects of a young person's life, which an adult might be able to pick up on. For example, there could be concern about doing certain events or activities (such as keeping up with school work, performance in school assignments or assessments, or social dynamics), feeling persistently restless or irritable, having trouble falling asleep or frequently waking up with nightmares, being easily fatigued, having difficulty concentrating, scaring or tearing up easily, and accumulating muscle tension. For generalised anxiety disorder to be diagnosed, the symptoms need to be present more often than not for 6 months or more. Should concerning behaviours persist for even a month or two, however, it can be beneficial to have a child assessed sooner, so supportive interventions can be implemented.

Seek the kinds of age-appropriate support that the child or teenager is open to, such as consulting with a mental health professional who specialises in working with children, or a school counsellor who the child feels comfortable working with. This can help with getting to the bottom of the personal challenges they might be facing, and supporting them to deal with triggering situations and problem-solving.

For a child or teenager, needing professional support is not something to feel ashamed of. Often, the skills learned in these early-life contexts can lead to valuable skills that can bolster a person's mental health for the rest of their lives.

Regarding the tools contained in this book, teenagers can use them straightforwardly, allowing each individual to explore what might be most helpful to them. Younger children might need a more imaginative, play-oriented approach. Seek out a specialist in children's mental health or resources specifically recommended for children.

chapter 4

Anxiety toolkit:
Mind

'You don't have to control your
thoughts, you just have to stop letting
them control you.' — **Dan Millman**

This chapter's stress toolkit:

Exercise 4.1   Identifying common themes of the anxious mind

Exercise 4.2   Name it to tame it

Exercise 4.3   Bring your mind into the present moment with a
quick anxiety turn-around

Exercise 4.4   Feed yourself with positivity

Exercise 4.5   Write it down (ideas for journaling)

 ur minds can perpetuate anxiety. Research shows that we spend almost half of our waking hours thinking about what is not going on in the present moment. This is made up of thousands of thoughts each day, most of which are negative.

Are we biased towards negativity?

According to the National Science Foundation, we think about 12,000–60,000 thoughts per day and about 80% of them are negative. This points to a negativity bias, which has evolved as part of our human experience so we can quickly notice and move away from danger. Paul Rozin and Edward Royzman introduced this concept in their 2001 paper, titled 'Negativity bias, negativity dominance, and contagion'. They hypothesised that both humans and animals pay more attention to negative experiences as a survival imperative. It is true that some amount of negativity or constructive criticism might propel us to greater achievements, but it is arguably not 80%. Anxiety and chronic anxiety are born out of this negativity. The result is living our lives with more vigilance, suspicion and stress than we need to, and losing focus on the positive things in our lives. Fortunately, we can turn around negativity with the help of the tools in this book.

This chapter focuses on our minds and ways to shift from chronic negativity to more consistent positivity. It starts by unpacking common themes of an anxious mind. Then, it offers a general toolkit to combat negativity, including naming thoughts and feelings, bringing our minds into the present moment, feeding ourselves with positivity, and writing practices for slowing down, sifting and sorting through the thinking processes that can fuel anxiety.

Exercise 4.1

Identifying common themes of the anxious mind

What does your mind come up with? Here are some common options. Are any familiar to you?

1. Past regrets

2. Dwelling on the past

3. Worry about the future

4. Self-criticism, self-doubt

5. Unhealthy comparisons, envy or jealousy

6. Blaming and shaming others

What are some other ways that your mind winds you up, or keeps you feeling unsettled or unsafe?

1. Past regrets

This includes 'if only' thinking, such as 'If only I had done this a little sooner.' Or 'If only I didn't do or say that.' 'Shoulds' and 'coulds' come into play here too, such as 'I should have or could have done or said this or that.' The result can be anxiety, frustration, anger, despair or depression, spiralling into negative thinking. Instead of dwelling on the past and wishing it had been different, a different approach is being willing to learn from the past.

2. Dwelling on the past

The contents of our thoughts include memories: some good and others troubling. We can dwell on both. This can be a source of negativity and stress. It's easy to see how memories of hurtful, challenging times can cause stress. But even the positive memories might be remembered as 'Those were the good old days', which we might long for to the detriment of our lives today. Enjoying our memories is a good thing. It only becomes a problem when our memories intrude on our ability to live in and appreciate the present. It can be like driving a car while looking only in the rear-view mirror. Clearly, this would be problematic.

3. Worry about the future

'What if' thinking comes into play here, together with a tendency towards snowball thinking or catastrophising about worst-case scenarios, which can build up. 'What if my presentation goes badly?' 'What if I lose my job because of it?' 'What if I don't have enough money to pay rent?' 'What if I lose my car and home and end up homeless, living on the streets or relying on my parents again?' And so on. When we follow these trains of thought, they can burrow us further into a dark tunnel of negativity. This thinking steals our attention away from the present moment and what we really need to focus on (such as preparing and practising well for the presentation, and seeking what support we need for it).

A useful remedy to play with is to answer each 'what if' question as it comes up. This can slow down and eventually stop a racing train of thought, opening us to our intelligence, reason and conscious choice. For even greater benefit, also consider what actions you can take from answering the 'what if' scenarios. Or you could start a train of thought in a positive direction. 'What if wonderful things happen' that you could word as you wish. Answering these questions can also be helpful and possibly revealing because of how you might discover fear of the positive and perhaps realise a need to prepare and open yourself to step into these positive scenarios. 'What if' thinking can be a useful tool to apply deliberately at times too, such as when assessing risks and considering different scenarios relating to future planning. Considering the answers to each 'what if' question encourages us to think more deeply through different options or courses of action towards making informed decisions.

4. Self-criticism, self-doubt

Here, we put ourselves down with degrading self-talk and 'not good enough' or 'what's wrong with me?' kinds of thinking. This could apply to anything from our abilities, choices and behaviour, to our basic goodness or how likeable, loveable or worthy we believe we are. We all tend to have an inner voice that can bring us down, as well as one that can lift us up.

You can try speaking with your inner voices to open up different perspectives. For example, you might speak to an inner critic with authority. With this, you can realise your inner critic only holds an opinion, not an absolute truth; you can consider other opinions too. Perhaps imagine your inner critic as an image or character, such as a witch, a tiny bossy person, a strict school teacher or whatever entertains you. This can help you separate from it and open the possibility for another part of yourself (hopefully one that is more supportive and helpful) to come forward. You might also consider how a friend would advise you, or what advice you would give a friend in your position – then take your own advice. We often are much kinder to others than we are to ourselves.

5. Unhealthy comparisons, envy or jealousy

Here, we might idealise others while making ourselves feel bad or 'less than' in comparison. Whether we are after a different body shape, intellect, relationship status or physical ability, there is always something to compare ourselves to. Used for the good, this can spur us on to become the person we wish to be, inspired by those we admire. Overused, it can be like a whirlpool sucking us into a spiral of negativity and possibly into depression. It can then be difficult to rise to the surface and remember who we really are – what our gifts are, what we have accomplished, and what we can feel grateful for. If this resonates with you, refer to the depression toolkit in chapters 7–11 for further support.

6. Blaming and shaming others

This involves placing all the responsibility for events and actions outside of ourselves, which can be disempowering. Sometimes these thoughts are valid and we are not always correct with our beliefs and assumptions. Dwelling on blaming and shaming others can keep a negative mindset in place, so working with this can be important. You might need to find bravery or be humble to own your part in a situation, which might also inspire others to do the same. You might also need to ask for help and reality-check your thoughts and beliefs. Through this, we might come to see a bigger picture perhaps pertaining to a person, a situation or ourselves.

General tools for taking on the anxious mind

No matter the theme that anxiety is feeding off in your mind, here are some general tools to help. Find what works best for you:

- Name it to tame it.
- Bring your mind into the present moment.
- Feed yourself with positivity.
- Write it down.

Exercise 4.2

Name it to tame it

Naming your feelings or thoughts can put a stop to anxiety's fixation on danger. This could be pausing to state, 'I am really anxious right now' or 'My head is spinning and I can't think straight'. The process of naming our experience can bring the prefrontal cortex back online – this part of the brain allows us to think in rational, considered, intelligent ways. Naming our feelings can also calm the amygdala, which is our brain's alarm system for danger. As a result our survival-based anxious freeze response can relax and we can more quickly find our way back to feeling in control. We are then better able to evaluate our situation and choose how to respond.

Exercise 4.3

Bring your mind into the present moment with a quick anxiety turn-around

Your attention is like a spotlight, shining awareness on whatever it focuses on. As the sayings go: 'Where your attention goes, energy flows,' or 'What you pay attention to will grow.' If you dwell on your thoughts, then your tendency to over-think will grow. If you turn your attention to the present moment, or to your goals and dreams and proactive steps towards them, then this is what will grow.

1. Where is your attention now?

To find out, experiment with your attention for a few moments. Zoom inwards to focus for a few moments on thoughts, feelings and body sensations. Now, open your attention outwards to the space around you. Perhaps imagine pouring attention out into your environment. You might notice sights, sounds and smells around you, or the temperature of the air, or something you can touch. Perhaps notice your surroundings with a wide, panoramic view. You might play with moving attention in and out of yourself, seeing what your preference is at this time. Maybe you prefer being inwardly focused, or maybe you prefer an outward, action- or interaction-oriented focus and feel less comfortable bringing attention inwards. You can also hold your attention half inside and half outside yourself. How easy is it for you to do this, to be aware of yourself and your feelings while also aware of your environment?

Playing with present-moment awareness can have a refreshing, potentially calming effect because it can interrupt habitual attention and thought patterns. You could simply pause now and then in your day to deliberately notice your surroundings. You could also place a post-it note in a visible place to remind you to do so. For a longer mindfulness practice designed to grow your ability to hold attention in the present moment, try the guided practice in Chapter 13, called 'Sharpen mental clarity and grow inner joy with mindfulness'.

2. Turn your attention outwards for a quick anxiety turn-around

As soon as you notice feeling anxious, deliberately turn your attention outwards to focus on your surroundings and what is going on around you. How long can you maintain this outward focus of attention? Challenge yourself to keep it up for 20–30 seconds at a time and notice how it leads you to feel. Perhaps your body relaxes a little and your mind clears. You can experiment with how this works for you as a quick anxiety turn-around.

3. Try it for social anxiety

Focusing your attention outwards can be an effective strategy with social anxiety, encouraging you to move out of your thoughts and assumptions about what people are thinking into real-time eye contact and conversation. This can put a stop, at least in the moment, to fixating on worries about being rejected or humiliated in some way. It also allows us to learn and grow from direct social experience. Any time we actively engage with and care for each other, our pets or even for our plants, it helps draw our attention out of habitual thinking and into the moment – and research shows this is good for health and longevity. Doing so can stimulate our relaxation response and boost a sense of heartfelt connectedness to each other and our lives.

Exercise 4.4

Feed yourself with positivity

Because we know that we humans tend to orient our minds towards the negative, to tip the scales we can benefit from emphasising the positives. Here are some ways to go about it:

- **Remind yourself of your good, beautiful qualities and achievements.** If you struggle with this, you might benefit from listing your positive qualities, compliments you have received and your achievements over the years.

- **Reframe 'I am worried' with 'I care'.** Health psychologist and lecturer at Stanford University, Dr Kelly McGonigal, makes this recommendation. It is based on the idea that we would not worry if we did not care, and that caring is usually a good thing. This reframing can bring kindness towards ourselves and open our hearts to what we are 'caring' about. It can counter that harsh inner critic. The kind, warm-hearted feelings it evokes also tap into our wholesome ventral vagus nerve to boost our capacity for resourceful, creative and compassionate thinking. Added to this, we put ourselves in a better position to prioritise what we care about. The result can be better management of our time and energy, and encouragement to let go of what is not important.

- **Notice beauty around you and what lights you up.** It could be something unexpected like the laugh of a child, the beauty of a flower or a smile exchanged with a stranger. It could be deliberately recalling a wonderful memory or thinking of one of your favourite people or pets. Absorb the good feelings for as long as you can, breathing them through your heart for a few uplifting moments.

- **Keep a gratitude journal.** Each day, try to identify at least three things you feel grateful for or appreciated from your day. These could be the smallest things, like that you have a roof over your head and food to eat, or bigger things like something wonderful or an achievement that happened. In this way, you can regularly combat negativity with daily reminders of the good things, which can warm your heart and feed into a more positive outlook.

Exercise 4.5

Write it down (ideas for journaling)

Holding thoughts, to-do lists and worries in our minds can be stressful. It can lead to our minds being overburdened by everything we have to remember. Always having a pen and paper handy, such as carrying a notebook with you or keeping some paper or post-it notes handy, can make a big difference to regularly clearing your mind. According to popular author Natalie Goldberg, 'whether you're keeping a journal or writing as a meditation, it is the same thing. What is important is you are having a relationship with your mind.'

Mental health benefits of journaling

Research has shown many mental health benefits of keeping up a writing practice, such as journaling, for up to 20 minutes a day. This includes improving emotional resilience and being a useful tool for problem-solving. Journaling helps us slow down and bring conscious awareness and coherence to our thinking process, helping to counteract the runaway nature of our minds. This can be especially useful when we feel anxious with fast-paced, repetitive, incoherent and fragmented thoughts. Because we can only write at a certain speed, our thinking process needs to slow down to accommodate it.

Some ideas for writing and journaling to try:

○ Keep a pen and paper handy to jot down your thoughts. It is up to you if you wish to write regularly or on a need-for basis.

○ Make shopping and to-do lists to help you keep a clear head.

○ Write down your worries. If you wish, follow this with identifying what you can do, or making a list of actions to take.

○ Brainstorm if you are planning for something, allowing your ideas to flow freely before ordering them and creating action items.

○ Write about a particular topic or problem that has been on your mind. The STEPS model in Chapter 15 can be helpful to guide your thinking.

○ Go with the flow to clear the contents of your mind onto the page.

○ Write or draw, filling the pages in whatever way works for you with words and images.

○ Write about your goals and dreams with a short- and long-term focus. Then keep up a weekly to-do list in line with this.

○ Write about your sanity and strengths. In this way, you can rewrite your life story to feel more empowering by focusing on what helped you survive or even thrive through challenging times. Writing in this way has been found to improve your sense of well-being as opposed to simply writing about what happened.

○ List your positive attributes, perhaps including compliments you have received over the years, achievements and everything you feel grateful about. If you struggle with this, you might ask for help from someone who knows and cares about you. Then keep this list for future reference – you are welcome to add to it as time goes by too.

chapter 5

Anxiety toolkit:
Breathing

'If I had to limit my advice on healthier living to just one tip, it would be simply to learn how to breathe better.' – **Andrew Weil, MD**

This chapter's stress toolkit:

 here is an inextricable link between breathing and anxiety. If you release the breathing pattern that goes with anxiety, you release the anxiety. From our body's perspective, it's that simple. Of course, our minds are strong and compelling, and it is not easy to let go of worries and narrations that can send us into a stress response. Life experiences can also be tumultuous. But if we give it a chance, we might discover

how effective breathing can be. Breathing taps directly into the autonomic nervous system, which is both the creator and potentially the remedy for our physical experience of anxiety. From there, a calmer, clearer state of mind and body open up to make us more discerning and mindful, no matter what might be going on.

This chapter offers accessible breathing methods for releasing the physical experience of anxiety. You are invited to try them out and find the techniques that work best for you. Give yourself time to get used to the practices, so you can surrender more fully to the process and reap the maximum mental, emotional and physical rewards. In this way, you can grow your breathing toolkit for life. Many of the practices can be used whenever you need to de-stress. Or you can stretch them out into longer practices when you wish to experience the benefits more deeply.

With all breathing practices, remember that thoughts will distract you as you go along. It is natural for your mind to wander, especially if you have a lot on your mind. Each time you notice this, direct your attention back to your breathing gently and with a smile. Doing so can be good practice for directing your attention away from worrisome thoughts and into a calmer, clearer state.

Breathing basics and a marker of health

Each time we inhale, the energising sympathetic nervous system is activated. Each time we exhale, the calming parasympathetic nervous system is activated. As a result, when we breathe in, our heart beats a little faster, and when we breathe out, our heart rate slows down a little. This is a natural phenomenon called heart rate variability (HRV). When we practise slower and steadier breathing, or lengthening our exhalations, our HRV increases, which is a marker of the body's resilience and health. Anxious, shallow and faster upper-chest breathing, which by default emphasises inhalations, reduces our HRV. It also creates body tension that prevents us from exhaling fully and letting go into relaxation. Many studies have shown a connection between slowed-down breathing and an immediate increase in HRV. This means we need to keep up our breathing practices and eventually shift habitual breathing patterns if we wish to sustain the results. All the practices in this chapter can guide you into more optimal HRV for health, resilience and well-being.

Exercise 5.1

A feel for anxious versus relaxed breathing

1. Draw your shoulders up slightly towards your ears. Begin to take short, shallow and fairly quick breaths into your upper-chest area. You can also play with holding or catching your breath while your upper body is tense in this way. Only continue for a few seconds because it may feel like too much quite quickly. How does it make you feel? This can be what anxiety feels like.

2. Drop your awareness down to your feet and release your shoulders, so you can feel more grounded. If you are sitting, you can also sit more evenly on your seat to centre and surrender into the stabilising pull of gravity. Notice how your breathing might slow down all on its own; you can invite your breathing to become even more slow and steady to nourish your nervous system. Breathe in and out through your nose (if you can), which can be more relaxing than breathing through your mouth.

3. Continue for three to five slow, deeper breaths. While doing so, you can add the following steps to increase the calming effect.

4. Scan your body from head to toe for tension, such as in your jaw, neck, shoulders and chest areas, then let it go.

5. With each slow in-breath, imagine using more of your lung capacity. Let your belly expand slightly as you breathe in. As you reach the top of your in-breath, allow your ribs to open and chest to gently expand. Keep your shoulders relaxed as you do so. On exhalation, relax your chest and at the very end, gently press your belly towards the spine to press out the last bit of air. Repeat three to five times, breathing in and out, in this slow, deep and full way.

6. Deepen the relaxation effect – experiment with lengthening your exhalations for as long as you comfortably can, so your exhalations

are longer than your inhalations. Perhaps use a mental count of four on inhalation and five or six on exhalation as you open to deeper relaxation.

7. Pause for a moment to notice how you feel. Perhaps you feel a bit calmer, or there might be some subtle buzzing in your head or body from the increased oxygenation and fresh boost of energy. This breathing pattern is the polar opposite to the shallow breathing that fuels anxiety.

Note: if you feel light-headed at any time while using a breathing practice, pause for a few moments and place a hand on the top of your head as if putting a lid on your light-headedness. Breathe naturally until you feel stabilised, then resume your practice perhaps more gently than before.

Best practices for breathing

The breathing exercise you have just completed contains an introduction to a few best practices for breathing that are scientifically validated. These can help to keep anxiety at bay and include:

- lengthening your exhalations
- nose breathing
- diaphragmatic breathing
- slow breathing.

Details about and exercises for these optimal breathing practices follow. The intention is to grow your ability to breathe more effectively and efficiently for all the potential benefits breathing brings to your mind, mood and body; stress resilience; and even your athletic abilities.

Exercise 5.2

Lengthening your exhalations for on-the-spot stress relief

1. A physiological sigh

When you are in the grips of anxiety, you might need a fairly strong breathing technique to help your body shift gears into relaxation and a calmer, clearer presence. A physiological sigh can be used for this. This is something we do involuntarily many times in a day, following our body's reflexive need to de-stress and restore equilibrium. It involves maximising the air we take into our lungs, sometimes with a double inhale, before releasing it in a long, sighing exhale. The long exhalation rids the lungs of excess carbon dioxide, which is a chemical compound associated with anxiety. In this exercise, you are invited to carry out this sigh voluntarily for stress relief. Take one to five of these breaths, or more if you like, until you feel a shift:

- Inhale in two parts. First, draw the breath into your belly, then pause for a moment before drawing air into your chest as much as you can without raising your shoulders. This allows your lungs to fill more fully with air and better oxygenate your body for a mini energy boost.

- Exhale by sighing or blowing your air out through your mouth as loudly as you feel comfortable and for as long as you can, while imagining breathing out your worries and troubles. You have now completed one round of the parasympathetic sigh. Repeat as many times as feels good, perhaps lengthening your exhalations for a bit longer with each sigh.

In general, sighing is our body's natural way to reset the autonomic nervous system when it has been activated. Whether reflexive or deliberate, sighing stimulates the vagus nerve and the calming parasympathetic nervous system. It can lead us to feeling more balanced and relaxed. Even one good, deep sigh can make a difference.

2. Sing, hum, read aloud, laugh out loud or have long conversations

All of these stimulate the calming, nourishing relaxation response that lets us rest and digest well while enhancing our ability to connect in sincere, heartfelt ways with each other. A piece of advice from Dr Stephen Porges: if you fear public speaking, aim to get one more word out with each exhalation than you usually would. This can have a calming effect on your nervous system to ease your fears.

Nose versus mouth breathing

The mouth and nose are not equal for breathing. Even though when your nose is blocked, your mouth can be helpful to inhale essential air, only the nose is properly designed to process and prepare the air for your lungs. The nose and its nasal cavities are designed to filter the air we breathe with fine nose hairs that capture dust, allergens, germs and pollen. Further back, air swirls through nasal passages to be warmed, humidified and further cleaned before entering the lungs.

> Only nose breathing produces nitric oxide. Nitric oxide is an important molecule for health. Its primary effect is vasodilation, or relaxation of the inner muscles of the blood vessels, causing them to widen and increase circulation. This is associated with the calming parasympathetic nervous system and improves the efficiency of the delivery of blood, nutrients and oxygen to every part of the body. It also reduces blood pressure.

Mouth breathing delivers cold, unfiltered air to the lungs in larger gulps than they can process. Mouth breathing is meant for speaking, laughing and sighing. But for breathing when we are at rest, nose breathing is best.

Experimenting with nose versus mouth breathing

Try this out for a moment. Open your mouth and take a few breaths, faster than your usual breathing. Notice how you feel. You might be reminded of the last time you were out of breath. When you breathe this way, it is actually a stress signal to your brain, associated with the fight or flight response. Now, close your mouth (provided your nose is not blocked) and take a few smooth, long breaths in and out through your nose. How do you feel now? Even if you were to breathe quickly through your nose, the amount of air you ingest is far less than through the mouth. This is because the nasal passages are narrower than the throat. Even though you take in less air with each breath, your body can utilise the air better because of the link between nose breathing and your relaxation response.

You might become curious about your breathing to find out how much you breathe through your nose or mouth during the day. Try encouraging yourself to keep your mouth closed whenever you are on your own, not eating and not speaking with others.

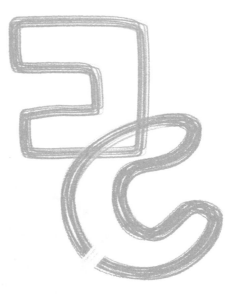

Exercise 5.3

Nose-breathing practices for calming and upliftment

1. Nose humming

A study by Eddie Weitzberg and Jon O.N. Lundberg has shown that humming while breathing through your nose (alternatively called nose humming) can increase nitric oxide levels 15-fold compared to normal quiet breathing. This means that our immunity, our blood circulation and the oxygenation of our vital organs are boosted through vasodilation and the health-promoting effects of nitric oxide, as mentioned earlier. So keep your anxiety at bay, your spirits lifted and your immunity boosted by humming your favourite tune whenever you get a chance!

2. Alternate nostril breathing (nadi shodhana)

Did you know that your nostrils alternate their workload through the day, with one nostril active usually for 2–4 hours at a time while the other takes a break? This is known as the nasal cycle, which involves alternating contraction and expansion inside of each nostril. Every minute of the day, our breathing moves through either one nostril or the other, with airflow mostly through one and a much smaller amount flowing through the other.

The alternate nostril breathing practice is a yogic technique that can have a balancing effect on our emotions, a clarifying effect on our minds and encourage relaxation. It can be used any time we can dedicate a few minutes to its practice, such as before going to sleep, when feeling emotional or before an important meeting. It can also have a balancing effect on the right and left brain hemispheres, helping to integrate our logical and creative aspects.

Use the thumb and ring finger of your right hand to press closed one nostril at a time. If you wish, you can rest your forefinger and middle finger in between your eyebrows to further encourage the centring of mind. Keep your shoulders and body relaxed as you practice.

- Breathe in as slowly as you can through your left nostril while your right thumb gently closes your right nostril.
- At the top of your in-breath, pause for a moment as you close your left nostril with your ring finger and release your thumb, then exhale slowly through your right nostril.
- Then breathe in through your right nostril, followed by closing your right nostril with your thumb and releasing your ring finger to breathe out through your left nostril. You have now completed one round of alternate nostril breathing.
- Repeat for 5–10 rounds.
- When completed, release your hands and arms to your sides or lap and take a few relaxed, slow breaths through both nostrils, noticing any shifts in how you feel after the practice.

Diaphragmatic breathing

The diaphragm is a large muscle that separates the belly from the chest. Breathing is optimised when initiated at the level of the diaphragm, which is alternatively known as belly breathing. This is because of how the belly naturally moves with this relaxed kind of breathing. Diaphragmatic breathing lets the lungs expand more fully on inhalation and empty more completely on exhalation, keeping the lungs ventilated, clean and healthy.

Compared to anxious breathing, diaphragmatic breathing lets your body absorb more air, oxygenating your body and brain more fully. It also provides a massage to your internal organs through the movement of the diaphragm and acts as a pump for lymphatic fluids to help keep your body healthy. This is how babies breathe when they are relaxed and how all of us breathe during deep sleep. It is also how we can train ourselves to breathe for the restorative, energising and grounding effect that it can have on our bodies and minds.

Are you breathing into your chest or diaphragm?

Place one hand in the middle of your chest and the other in the middle of your belly. Notice which of your hands moves the most with each round of breathing. Now, encourage your belly to gently expand with each inhalation and relax with each exhalation. For fullest breathing, you might experience your in-breath in two parts: first expanding your belly, and then drawing upwards to expand your ribs and open your chest. The exhalation is simply a release and relaxing of the air out of your body, perhaps with a slight pressing of your navel towards your spine at the end of exhalation to squeeze out the last bit of air. When you are relaxed, breathing can settle into its own quiet, internal rhythm.

Exercise 5.4

Slow diaphragmatic breaths for an energy boost

At any time during your day, take 5–10 slow and full deep breaths, using a mental count of five or six on inhalation and exhalation, respectively. Breathe in from belly to chest and when you breathe out, at the end of exhalation gently press your belly towards your spine to release the last bit of air. Aim to smooth the transitions between inhalation and exhalation so breathing in and out feels seamless and circular.

You can also experiment with pausing for a moment after both inhalation and exhalation. In this way, you can give yourself a subtle energy boost from the increased oxygen from breathing slowly and deeply. Remember to keep your body relaxed, especially avoiding raising your shoulders while inhaling so you can increase relaxation.

Slow breathing

As stress responses like fight, flight and anxiety take hold inside of us, the sympathetic nervous system is activated, speeding up our heart and breathing rates. Breathing slowly on purpose is a way to hack into our nervous system and re-route stress from sped-up sympathetic activation to the slowed-down calm of parasympathetic dominance. Deliberately slowing down breathing has been understood for centuries as a path to greater personal mastery over the mind and body. This is seen in age-old physical arts such as qigong and yoga. It is also inherent in the chanting and singing traditions found in many religions, which naturally encourage deeper breathing and can induce states of deep calm.

When breathing slows down, so do our heart rate and stress levels as we slip into our nourishing relaxation response. Ideally, this slowed-down breathing falls into a sweet spot rhythm of about 5 seconds per inhalation and 5 seconds per exhalation. This slow rate of breathing is considered particularly beneficial to our health and happiness, and has been given a name of its own: resonance frequency or coherent breathing.

Resonance frequency breathing

Resonance frequency breathing refers to slow, relaxed, diaphragmatic breathing at about three to seven breaths per minute. This is in contrast to the average adult breathing rate of between 12 and 20 breaths per minute. Breathing slowly, even for just a few minutes, can have a regulating effect on the nervous system by triggering the relaxation response. It can also create synchrony between our heart rate, breathing and circulation in a way that can feel soothing and be beneficial to health. For example, it is found to lower blood pressure, increase oxygen delivery throughout the body and, with regular practice, improve quality of sleep. It can also ease anxiety and be uplifting from depression.

Exercise 5.5

Resonance frequency breathing

To experience resonance frequency breathing, try the simple practice that follows, ideally breathing through your nose on inhalation and exhalation (if you can). Breathing is smooth and continuous between inhalation and exhalation.

1. Inhale by sipping in air slowly through your nose for a mental count of five (or 5 seconds). Exhale by breathing out for the same smooth, quiet count of five. This is one round of resonance frequency breathing.

2. Continue for five rounds. Experts recommend that if you placed a feather under your nose while using this practice, you would aim to have your breathing be so minimal and light that the feather would be undisturbed.

3. Once your rounds are complete, take a few moments to notice how your body feels, and enjoy the stillness and focus that it can bring. You can do this at any time of day or night for a calming break.

Note that it may take a little while to get used to this slowed-down, very light breathing. With practice, it does become more familiar and can lead you to experience its promised calm, settling effects. To help, you could add the following:

Ujjayi breathing

This is a breathing technique from the yogic tradition. It is a soothing, centring breathing practice for slowing down and smoothing out your breathing. It involves breathing in and out through your nose, but instead of breathing lightly and quietly at the pace of resonance frequency breathing, you slightly close the back of your throat to limit the amount of air you breathe, so it makes an ocean-like sound in the back of your throat. As you breath in and out, you hear a gentle 'hhhhhhhh' sound.

As you become familiar with the pace of resonance frequency breathing, you could perhaps start taking a few Ujjayi breaths then move on to some really light and quiet resonance frequency breaths.

Movement coordinated with breathing

Another way to support yourself in breathing more slowly without building up tension in the body is to practise slow movements coordinated with breathing. This is what movement arts such as qigong and yoga are all about; essentially, they are breathing practices that use mindful movement to expand your ability to absorb vital energy, which is believed to be carried by the breath. In a sitting or standing position, you might experiment with raising your arms up like wings on each slow inhalation then lowering your arms gradually and gracefully down to your sides on each slow exhalation. The intention is to move slowly and coordinate breath with movement. Movement can help to minimise distraction and smooth out any shakiness that might accompany stress and anxiety.

When you have 15–20 minutes, there is a guided movement sequence in Chapter 14 that naturally encourages resonance frequency breathing and peace of mind.

Is carbon dioxide just a waste product in breathing?

Experts such as Patrick McKeown are at the forefront of debunking the myth that CO_2 is only a waste product to be expelled from the body. This has come with the discovery that when we take in less air, such as when we breathe slowly and lightly, and increase our ability to hold our breath for longer, there are two coinciding effects. The concentration of CO_2 is higher in the body and there is better O_2 delivery to the body's muscles, vital organs and cells. This is beneficial to our energy levels and health.

This harks back to what is called the Bohr effect, which Danish physiologist Christian Bohr discovered in 1904. The Bohr effect refers to the vital role that CO_2 plays in delivering and releasing O_2 to the parts of the body that need it. According to Bohr, 'The carbon dioxide pressure of the blood is to be regarded as an important factor in the inner respiratory metabolism. If one uses carbon dioxide in appropriate amounts, the oxygen that was taken up can be used more effectively throughout the body.'

Tips for slow-breathing and breath-holding practices

1. Always work within your capabilities and don't push yourself beyond what feels comfortable.

With resonance frequency breathing, for example, this might mean working up over time to 5 seconds per inhalation and 5 seconds per exhalation, and being patient with yourself in the process, knowing that it will become easier and feel more natural with practice.

2. Meet the sensation of air hunger with a smile.

When you meet air hunger during a breathing practice, try smiling. Smiling can soften the sense of panic you may feel and encourage withstanding air hunger for a few moments longer, knowing it can be good for your health and anxiety resilience. Smiling sends a message to the brain that this activity is safe and can be trusted. As you become used to the sensation, it will become easier and will feel more natural. At the same time as smiling, resist the urge to gasp for air. Instead, keep your body relaxed as you breathe in smoothly through your nose (if you can). Inviting your body to relax as opposed to tensing up in panic can help to gradually increase our capacity for slower, more oxygen-efficient breathing. We might also realise that, even if we cannot get rid of the triggers for anxiety in our lives, we can improve our ability to tolerate anxiety and meet it with a smile.

3. Take a break if you need to.

During slow-breathing and breath-holding practices, if air hunger were ever to get too great, just pause and catch your breath with a few natural or deep breaths through your nose before resuming the practice.

Holding your breath for a boost to energy and anxiety resilience

Without training, the average person can hold their breath for up to 30 seconds before gasping for air. Elite athletes in breath-holding, such as free divers, can train their ability to hold their breath for 10 minutes. It is possible for all of us to increase our tolerance for holding our breath. Doing this can boost our energy levels in ways that are good for blood circulation, oxygenation of our tissues and cells, and providing a wonderful experience of energy pulsing throughout our body. This is caused by the higher levels of carbon dioxide achieved when we practise breath-holding and slow breathing.

Air hunger and the suffocation reflex

Air hunger is the feeling of not having enough air to breathe. It can happen when carrying out breathing practices that ask us to slow down or hold our breath. Air hunger can cause intense anxiety or panic associated with a life-or-death fear of not being able to breathe. This is called the suffocation reflex and is a primal fear triggered by a cluster of neurons, called central chemoreceptors, located at the base of the brain stem. This is different from when we feel threatened by something in our environment, which is a fear triggered in the emotional brain centre, the amygdala.

Breathing practice as exposure therapy for anxiety

Studies have shown how we can grow our tolerance for the intense anxiety or panic caused by the suffocation reflex. (Only to a point because, of course, we don't actually want to suffocate.) This is helpful because it can be such an effective body-based tool for building stress and anxiety resilience.

One researcher focusing on the correlation between carbon dioxide and the suffocation reflex is Justin Feinstein, a clinical neuropsychologist at the University of Iowa, USA. Feinstein makes use of inhaled carbon dioxide as a trigger for anxiety and panic in a controlled setting, for the purpose of increasing tolerance for these intense feelings. This is a kind of exposure therapy because it simulates anxiety or panic, and offers a way to build resilience through repeated exposure. This is the same principle behind applying a breathing technique, such as slow or held breathing, that increase our carbon dioxide levels and thus can increase our tolerance for both air hunger and anxiety.

Breath-holding practices for a boost to energy and anxiety resilience

Here are three simple ways to play with holding your breath so you can experience the energising potential for yourself. Breathe in and out through your nose if you can.

Important note: holding your breath is not advised when pregnant or with certain medical conditions. If you do have a medical condition, such as one that affects your lungs or heart, please consult with your primary doctor before trying out new practices like these. When you do begin, go really easy with the practice, opting for just a second or two of breath-holding to start with. Alternatively, there are many other methods contained in this book that you can safely work with.

Exercise 5.6

Box breathing

This is a simple introduction to breath-holding that can be great for reducing anxiety and increasing energy levels with just a few rounds of breathing. Breathing is all through your nose if possible.

- Breathe in for a slow mental count of four.
- Hold your breath at the top of the inhalation for the same count of four.
- Breathe out for the count of four.
- Hold your breath at the end of exhalation for a count of four.
- Repeat 1–10 times.
- Resume normal breathing and notice how you feel.

Exercise 5.7

Breath-holding while walking

This practice is inspired by the Buteyko breathing method and is recommended for adults in relatively good health.

- Breathe in and out through your nose (if you can) then hold your breath towards the end of exhalation. You don't need to empty your lungs completely, at least to start with, to help you hold your breath in this exhaled way. With time, you can experiment with letting as much air out as possible before holding your breath.

- Note that holding your breath at the end of an exhalation stimulates the calming parasympathetic as opposed to the activating sympathetic nervous system, which would be stimulated if you held your breath at the top of an inhalation.

- Walk as many steps as you can while holding your breath. Anders Olsson, author of *Conscious Breathing* suggests counting the number of steps you can take before needing to take a breath (and without pushing yourself to the point of air desperation). Over time, you aim to increase the number of steps you can take while holding your breath.

- Inhale when you need to, resisting the urge to gasp for air. Instead, keep your body calm as you breathe in smoothly through your nose (if you can). Inviting your body to relax from the inside (especially your throat, shoulders, chest and belly areas as well as your hands or anywhere else you might notice tension) can help with breath-holding.

- Take a few natural recovery breaths. Walk and breathe normally (still through your nose if you can) for 30 seconds to 1 minute to recover.

- Repeat the cycle of breath-holding and recovery time while walking. Do this as many times as you wish. Perhaps start with five cycles during a walk and, over time, increasing to 20 minutes or your entire walk.

- Notice the effect on your mind and energy levels.

Note: High-performance Olympic athletes have used breath-holding during athletic events and won gold medals. But it is not for everyone. There are other methods to try while exercising, including lengthening exhalations such as using Carl Stough's breathing coordination techniques, which also apply to the cultivation of health and well-being. Or you could simply practise slowed-down, rhythmic breathing to a mental count where your breathing is in rhythm with your movement.

Exercise 5.8

Relaxing 4–7–8 breathing

This yogic breathing technique has grown in popularity and become associated with Dr Andrew Weil, who highly recommends it. It can act like a natural tranquilliser for the nervous system. It can be helpful with falling asleep and waking up refreshed, as well as with soothing and releasing our worries by imagining breathing them out with each long exhalation. It is based on a yogic breathing practice involving breath-holding and lengthened exhalations. According to Dr Weil, the most important phase of 4–7–8 breathing is holding your breath. It is at this time that oxygen circulation and absorption throughout the body increases most.

- Sit with your body in a comfortable upright position rather than leaning back if you can, or if you need to, lean back but prop yourself upright with cushions. You can also use this practice lying in bed, such as just before sleep or if you wake up in the middle of the night.

- Note that the ratio of 4–7–8 is more important than the specific amount of time, or how slowly or quickly you move through your mental counting. Because of this, you can play around with moving through this breathing practice more quickly or slowly to find the timing that works best for you.

- Place the tip of your tongue on the roof of your mouth behind your upper front teeth and keep it there for the duration of the exercise.

- Inhale through your nose for a mental count of four with your mouth closed.

- Hold your breath for a mental count of seven.

- Exhale slowly, blowing the air out your mouth, for a mental count of eight.

- Repeat at least three times, or for a few minutes, until you feel sufficiently relaxed. Aim to release tension from your body, especially while exhaling, and keep your insides relaxed, especially during breath-holding (particularly noting your jaw, neck, shoulders, chest and belly areas as well as relaxing your arms and hands). For building familiarity with this practice and potentially improving its effectiveness, for example in helping you fall asleep, use this practice for 5 days in a row while lying in bed to lull you to sleep.

Unconscious versus conscious breath-holding

Do you hold your breath or breathe shallowly when deeply engrossed in working or playing on your computer, iPad or smartphone? Research has found that we can slip into periods of barely breathing or breath-holding for about 30 seconds at a time when actively working on a screen. This might be while emailing, writing, texting or focusing for periods of time on computer-based work. Along with unconscious breath-holding can come physical rigidity from sitting still for an extended time.

Email apnoea

A former executive at Apple and Microsoft, Linda Stone, carried out a study into this phenomenon. Stone became curious through her own experience while engaging with emails. She wanted to look into how widespread this breathing issue was. Over a period of six months, Stone studied workers sitting in front of computers. She found that four out of five people held their breath or breathed shallowly while checking emails in particular. Stone coined the term 'email apnoea', which likens this phenomenon to sleep apnoea. This is because there are similar detrimental effects found to health and oxygen supply to the brain and vital organs, such as shown in research by Dr Margaret Chesney and Dr David Anderson through the National Institute of Health.

Rather than this being a cause for anxiety, it can have a depressing effect on the nervous system similar to a dissociated or blank, numb freeze response. Even though we can remain highly engaged mentally, our heart, breathing and metabolic rates can slow down significantly, leaving us feeling out of touch with and emotionally disconnected from our bodies. This is different from conscious breath-holding, which is beneficial to health. For ideas to counteract this modern-day condition, refer to the breathing-based toolkit for depression in Chapter 9.

chapter 6

Anxiety toolkit:
Body

'There is a surprising connection between posture and resilience.' **– Pat Ogden, founder of the Sensorimotor Psychotherapy Institute**

This chapter's stress toolkit:

e all know how good we can feel after exercising and sometimes during exercising too (unless we have pushed ourselves too hard). Exercising can open up our breathing and help us to feel more alive and stronger in ourselves. It can also ease anxiety during physical exertion and for about an hour or so afterwards. This body-based toolkit is for the time between exercising. These practices are life skills rather than a physical exercise program. The tools give us ways to regularly ease, soothe and release tension that can build up from anxiety and generally through the day. The tools also align us with our best selves, helping us remain calmer, clearer, happier and stress-resilient more consistently.

There are different ways to tap into the body as a resource when feeling anxious. You are invited to try out the practices of this chapter in your own time to discover what might work best for you. Also, there is a 15–20 minute 'Movement sequence to release tension and replenish energy' in Chapter 14. This can consolidate your physical ability to keep anxiety at bay while further honing your relaxation response. In these embodied ways, you can grow your ability to shift from stress into calmer clarity, sometimes in a matter of seconds.

Exercise 6.1

A sense of the raw data of stress and anxiety in your body

To get a sense of how tension can build up inside you, take a moment to recall a time when you felt stressed or anxious. Maybe you feel it now. Notice how your body responds. Do your chest and throat tighten up to restrict your breathing? Or does tension grip you in your belly? Do your shoulders tense up or does your neck feel tight? Does a furrow creep onto your brow? Do you hold your whole body rigidly? Without awareness, we can carry this tension with us through periods of the day, and sometimes for days and weeks at a time. This is the body's raw data of anxiety – we can also tap into this raw data to help us unwind from anxiety.

To experiment with turning this raw data around, extend your spine so you rise to your full height. Hold your head high and let your breathing naturally become fuller as a result. Notice how these simple physical adjustments might shift something in how you think and feel. What do you notice? Some describe a boost to their inner strength and determination, or a reminder to stand into their intelligence or logic, as opposed to being swept away in emotions or stress reactivity. Or you could feel more centred, discerning and decisive. This can be a quick way to upgrade the quality of our thinking so we can better assess what is real, what is possible and what we choose to do next. It also points to the strong connection between the body and mind. If you change one, the other changes along with it.

Some people prefer a bottom-up approach like this, starting with physical interventions and allowing the body to naturally encourage a change of mind. Others might prefer a top-down approach, starting with the mind (such as drawing on the mind toolkit for anxiety in Chapter 5) and consolidating with body-based skills. Use what works best for you.

This chapter's body-based toolkit is divided into the following categories, representing particular kinds of interventions:

- Catch it.
- Rise above it.
- Soothe it.
- Release it.
- Grow your ability to be with emotions that might lie under anxiety.
- Top up regularly with self-supportive touch to keep anxiety at bay.
- Walk for stress relief and emotional release.

You can use these interventions in any order. Experiment with what works best for you. Some of the exercises are intended for use on-the-spot and others for when you have more time.

Catch it

Paying more attention to your body and how it holds stress and anxiety can help you to be quicker in doing something about it. Later in this chapter, in exercises 6.7 and 6.8, you'll also find opportunities to catch and tune into emotion/s that might lie underneath anxiety for growing tolerance for being with your feelings and the relief this brings.

Exercise 6.2

Know your body's tension hotspots

Usually, we hold tension in particular areas of our bodies, such as in our shoulders, jaw, neck, upper back, eyes or belly. What are your tension hotspots? Where do you get aches or tightness regularly? It can be helpful to become familiar with these areas. You might create a habit of scanning your body from head to toe (or toe to head) at points throughout the day to pick up on these areas. Then you can make a point of easing up the areas and adjusting your posture to feel more centred and comfortable. You might also notice how your state of mind shifts along with your posture.

Rise above it

Here is an invitation to stand into your best self – align your posture with your values for the anxiety relief and confidence boost this can provide.

Exercise 6.3

Rise up to your full height and align with a bigger picture

Posture can be an important tool for reducing anxiety and building stress resilience. This is because posture organically reflects our thoughts and feelings. For example, when we feel down or ashamed, our posture tends to stoop. When we feel relaxed and happy, our posture is more upright and open. Experiment with this for a few moments. Stoop your posture and try to feel happy. Then stand tall with head high while trying to feel sad. How did that go? Our posture can override our thoughts and feelings because of stronger biofeedback and more nerve connections running from body to brain than from brain to body. It is like the body can trick the mind into feeling differently. With increased body awareness, we can come to realise how our posture can either perpetuate or remedy anxiety, depending on how we hold ourselves.

The physical gesture of rising to our full height and choosing to align with something bigger, like a bigger picture of a situation, or a higher or wiser aspect of ourselves, can send a strong signal to the brain and nervous system that we are in control. This reassurance can open our breathing to feel freer and boost our confidence to face our challenges.

Here are a few suggestions for rising above stress or anxiety:

1. Stand or sit tall

- Elongate your spine so your head is held high, while remaining comfortable rather than strained in your posture. To feel grounded, place your feet evenly on the ground or centre yourself over your sitting bones. Standing or sitting tall in this grounded way can feel physically and emotionally stabilising, and boost confidence when you might need it. You might try out this technique before an important meeting or whenever anxiety spikes and you want to feel more in control of your responses.

2. Imagine aligning with something inspiring

Here are a few ideas for visualising this:

- Imagine standing into your higher, wiser self.
  - + As you stand tall, you can imagine becoming a better, wiser version of yourself, or aligning with a bigger picture or higher perspective in a way that resonates with you.

- 'Pull yourself towards yourself.'
  - + Carrying out what this saying suggests might inspire you to centre yourself and stand taller, so you can think more clearly and align with your values.

- Stand tall between earth and sky.
  - + This is an invitation to place your uprightness or verticality within the natural context of the earth below and sky above. It can instantly shift your attention out of worries and into a sense of connection with something bigger, more universal and nature-based to inform your decision-making.
  - + Start by placing both feet evenly on the ground (even if wearing shoes). Imagine being supported and stabilised from below by the earth. While feeling grounded in this way, let your spine and posture lengthen and reach upwards through the crown of your head towards the vast, open sky. This image of being held between earth and sky draws on millennia-old wisdom from Eastern cultures that use simple practices like this to align with universal values for positive influence. It encourages good posture in a grounded way while also potentially opening our minds to see the bigger picture. We can thus steer our actions in inspiring, meaningful directions. Feeling held in this natural context can also offer a sense of emotional containment.

Soothe it

Here is an invitation to comfort yourself when anxiety rises up while nourishing your nervous system through self-supportive touch. There is a direct link between our skin and nervous system that develops from the same tissue in-utero. Supportive touch can feel like tonic for our nervous system. It can also shift us biochemically by releasing oxytocin in a matter of seconds. Oxytocin has been nicknamed our 'snuggle or cuddle' hormone; it is associated with feelings of relaxation and intimacy with ourselves and each other. Skin is also a natural protective boundary that separates what lies inside and outside of us. Caring and soothing touch can remind us of this to enhance our sense of emotional containment and safety. This can have a calming effect on feelings like anxiety, fear and overwhelm.

Exercise 6.4

On-the-spot self-soothing

Here are ways you can draw on self-supportive touch to soothe your nerves and stimulate your relaxation response:

1. Stroke your own arm or hand, or place a hand where it hurts.

You might rub your arm, neck, shoulders or lower back for some welcome soothing. You can also place a hand where it hurts, holding and warming the area or rubbing it for some targeted comfort. If you are around people, you can be inconspicuous by holding or stroking your own hand for some tactile soothing.

2. Place a hand on the centre of your chest.

Use a pressure that feels just right for you. Some like an open hand on the chest, while others prefer a fist for firmer support. You could also rub in a circular motion over the area to stimulate the emotionally soothing acupressure point located there.

Release it

This includes ways to unstick and let go of body tension, which can accumulate from stress and anxiety. Interventions can be used on-the-spot when you feel you need it. They also potentially open us to being more grounded, centred and energised. Explore the various options that follow to discover what you enjoy most. Then use your favourite methods regularly to keep up with stress release and encourage relaxation.

Exercise 6.5

Shake it out

Shake out parts of your body that feel tight or rigid. Shaking can be excellent to release excess energy from your nervous system. Here are some ways to go about it:

Go with the flow.

You can free flow with shaking out parts of your body from head to toe. Also, whenever you naturally might shudder or shake, you can let it naturally pass through your body to completion instead of stopping it. This can facilitate the natural release of pent-up energy.

Shake in an organised way.

For example, you might shake out your hands and arms for a few moments, then your shoulders, hips and neck (being careful not to hurt your neck). You can follow this with shaking out each of your legs in turn (holding on for balance if you need to).

Shake out tension through your tailbone.

This is an age-old practice that can be practised sitting or standing with both feet on the ground for stability. You can use it any time during the day to energise your spine, as well as last thing at night, as you let go of any thoughts or dramas from the day. It involves imagining that you have a tail and that your tailbone extends into this tail, which might look like a long dinosaur tail reaching down to the ground behind you. Shake out your hips as if wagging this tail from side to side a few times or as long as feels good. It can feel energising from the ground up and is a great way to take a break after you have been sitting for a while.

Exercise 6.6

Energise your posture and release blocked energy with gentle movements

In a break in your day, especially after you have been sitting and concentrating for a while, any one or a combination of these practices can be energising as well as physically and emotionally freeing. You can do them sitting or standing:

Pandiculating

Also known as a body yawn, pandiculation is driven by the urge to stretch out the body when yawning. It is nature's way of waking up the body to help with the transition from rest or sleep into action. Pandiculating can stretch out our spine and limbs, which increases blood circulation and lubricates our tissues and joints to help our bodies get moving more comfortably. Animals do it instinctively, indulging in a good wake-up stretch from top to tail.

As humans, we can benefit from being more thorough with it. It can be excellent for unsticking tension first thing in the morning, or any time you wish to loosen up your body. Give yourself a minute or two to organically follow where your body wishes to stretch out while yawning, perhaps reaching into your arms, twisting your spine, and even stretching into your lower back and legs. Follow this yawning, stretching impulse until it feels complete and your body feels more stretched out and ready to move. It can feel stabilising to place your two feet on the ground and centre yourself for a moment before moving into your day.

Neck rolling

Draw figure-8s with your nose in the air in front of you, letting your head and neck move with it as much as your body will allow to release neck tension. Move slowly to bring consciousness to your movement and not hurt your neck. Carry out three to nine nose figure-8s in one direction and then the other. You can play with bigger and smaller movements, depending on your range of motion.

Slouching and un-slouching your spine

Pause now and again to deliberately alternate between slouching and elongating your spine. This can invite you to return to your work with a more upright, centred and energised posture. Coordinate movement with breathing, exhaling when moving into a slouch and inhaling when elongating your spine. Repeat three to nine times for an energising effect that is excellent for spinal health too.

Shoulder rolling

Roll your shoulders backwards and forwards a few times to open your chest and release tension in the shoulders and upper back. You can also alternate rolling one shoulder then the other in a cycling kind of motion.

Hip rolling

You can play with tilting your pelvis or hips backwards and forwards, which you can do while sitting or standing. Repeat three to nine times. You can also circle your hips in one direction and the other a few times. When we sit for long periods of time, our hip area can lock into rigidity, which can lead to lower-back discomfort. Hip rolling can also have an energising effect on your spine as a whole. Sitting on a gym ball can be great for this.

Grow your ability to be with emotions that might lie under anxiety

Exercise 6.7

Tune into emotions that might lie underneath anxiety

When you notice you are anxious, try pausing and asking yourself what emotions might be with you underneath the anxiety. Dropping into these feelings can be relieving, especially if we have been resisting our feelings. Touching into our truth in this way can release endorphins, our body's natural painkillers, especially with tender emotions like sadness, to provide soothing relief. It may not be easy to open to our feelings. The earlier exercise for on-the-spot self-soothing can assist with growing our capacity to be with our feelings supportively, instead of being afraid of or resisting them. Different emotions can point to different needs we might have in the moment, for example:

- **Anger** A need to set a boundary, speak up or take action. Or use the fiery energy of anger to go out and seek support to help deal with a situation.

- **Sadness** Asks us to open our hearts and allow ourselves to be touched and moved by life, ideally with kindness. The skill of compassion and self-compassion, as described in Exercise 10.2 of the depression toolkit, can be helpful here. If sadness sinks into chronic melancholy, low motivation and emotional numbness, then refer to the depression toolkit in chapters 7–11 for further support.

- **Fear** Consider what you really are afraid of and if you can do something about it. If you can, it is important to do so. Or you may need to let go of what no longer applies. Reassurance might be helpful, such as reminding yourself you are safe and okay now. You can then go on to the 'soothe it' or 'release it' exercises in this chapter or the mind toolkit for anxiety in Chapter 4 to challenge the thought processes that might be fuelling your fear.

Exercise 6.8

Feel it to heal it

We humans might never be able to be rid of stress and anxiety. They are part of our survival hardwiring. The same goes for emotions, which are an integral part of life and relationships. So we might as well become better at living with them. From ancient mindfulness principles and practices to more recent psychological techniques, this is a well-validated approach. Instead of resisting our feelings, we practise turning towards them and gradually growing our ability to tolerate them.

Next time you feel anxious or emotional, you might pause for a few moments to simply notice how it is showing up in you, such as in your thoughts, body sensations and breathing. Turning to observe feelings and how they show up in your body and mind can stop negative thinking snowballing. With practice, you can grow your tolerance for your feelings and so increase your stress resilience.

Systematically desensitising yourself

Psychiatrist Joseph Wolpe developed an evidence-based therapy approach to working with phobias and anxiety disorders that draws on this principle. Called Systematic Desensitization, it is a kind of exposure therapy with three main parts. The first involves teaching muscle relaxation to increase our endurance of feelings and reduce fear reactivity. The second is listing all our fears and ranking them in terms of intensity, from least to worst anxiety-provoking. The third is to gradually expose ourselves to increasing intensities of our fears over time.

The purpose is to build tolerance for difficult feelings so when we experience them, they no longer debilitate us and we can live more confidently. No matter what emotions might come up, when we resist them, we tend to increase worrisome thinking and avoidant behaviours. This can create more problems for us than what we might be resisting. If we can learn to turn towards our feelings, however, we can discover that all feelings pass eventually and that there might be no need to fear them. Only when we are in touch with our feelings can we know what is really going on for us and consider what will be helpful towards our healing and growth.

Top up regularly with self-supportive touch to keep anxiety at bay

Exercise 6.9

Daily self-massage 'shower'

This is a longer supportive touch sequence that you can carry out when you have 5 minutes or longer. Practised once a day for a while, it can set a tone for your day of greater ease and calm. This sequence can feel like washing your body in the shower, providing you with a good dose of the nervous system's nourishment. Use this sequence any time you like, such as first thing in the morning or in a gap in your day. If practising just before bed, you can switch to the bedtime soothing option that follows.

Starting position

You can stand or sit. If standing, start with legs a comfortable or hip distance apart with feet parallel. Knees are relaxed or slightly bent so you feel grounded. If you need to sit, you can adapt this massage 'shower' to where your arms can reach in the seated position (such as brushing hands down the sides instead of the backs of your legs).

1. Belly rub

- Place both hands flat over your navel with one on top of the other; the thumbs may naturally overlap.
- Use your hands to draw clockwise circles around your navel three to nine times. Make smaller and bigger circles around your navel so your whole belly area receives a massage.

2. Chest and arm rub

- Keeping your left hand on your belly, raise your right hand to rub in circles over the centre of your chest three to nine times.

- Still using your right hand, rub three to nine circles at the top left corner of your chest (where your chest and shoulder meet).

- Raise your left arm up in front of you with palm facing upwards. Brush your right hand down the inside of your left arm all the way to your open palm and fingertips. Then flip your left arm so the palm faces downwards and brush your right hand up the outside of your left arm (from fingertips to the outside of your left shoulder).

- Bring your right hand back to the centre of your chest and place your left hand on top of your right hand for a centring moment.

- Then lower your right hand to your belly and, with your left hand, repeat the chest rubbing and the wiping down and up of the right arm. End by bringing both hands together again, one on top of the other over the centre of your chest, for a centring moment.

3. Lower back rub

- Bring hands down to your lower back (with right hand on the right side and left hand on the left side of your lower back).

- Give your lower back a rub, circling your hands three to nine times over the area so both sides of your lower back receive support in a way that feels good.

4. Leg sweep

- With your hands still on your lower back, take a deep breath in.

- Exhale as you brush your hands down the backs of your legs, bending your knees for comfort as you bend over your legs.

- Continue to brush your hands around the outsides of your feet.

- Inhale as you brush your hands up the insides of your feet and legs and over the front of your hips, gradually extending your legs and unfolding your spine to upright. Then meet your hands in a prayer pose in front of your chest.

- Exhale, bringing your hands down to your lower belly, just below your navel with one on top of the other. Soften into your knees so you feel grounded through your feet.

5. Repeat or close with three breaths

- If you wish, repeat two or three times.
- To close, take three deep, slow breaths into and out of your lower belly area. Then release your hands and step out into your day.

Note: For the leg sweep, if you cannot bend all the way down to your feet with legs bent, it is okay to reach just as far as you can go. Circle your hands as if drawing a circle in the air around the outsides and insides of your feet before making contact with your legs again, perhaps at knee level, or wherever you can comfortably reach.

Exercise 6.10

Bedtime soothing with self-supportive touch

Here are some ways you can hold your body for soothing effect when you are ready to go to sleep. These can draw attention out of your thoughts and into your body. You can use these positions while lying in bed, or if you wake up at night and wish to fall back to sleep.

1. Gently hold chest and belly.

- Place one hand flat on the centre of your chest and the other flat on your belly. Hold for 10 breaths using slow, belly breathing that inflates your belly and chest on inhalation then relaxing your body with each exhalation, imagining any stress and tension leaving your body. Breathe through your nose if you can.

2. Hold your head.

- Lie on your bed with hands cupped behind your head at the neck for 3–10 natural breaths, or you can aim to slow down your breathing with each breath. Breathe through your nose if you can.
- Move one hand to your forehead for a few more comforting breaths. You are also welcome to hold anywhere else on your head that feels good, such as holding the sides of your head or with one hand behind your head and the other covering your forehead.
- As you hold your head, absorb warmth and soothing from your hands as your attention might slip naturally from thinking into the warm, soft space of your body. Allow yourself to let go and feel heavier into the support of your bed to encourage deeper relaxation.

3. Self-hug with two options.

- Hands slipped under your armpits to hold the sides of your chest.
- Arms crossed over your chest with hands resting flat against opposite sides of your chest and fingers either under your collarbone or reaching slightly higher over your shoulders, wherever feels best.
- Hold for as long as feels good and soothing while breathing naturally.

4. Rest hips on backs of hands.

- If you can comfortably do so, slip your hands under your hips with palms down and allow your hips to rest on your hands for a few natural or slow breaths. This position can be helpful to quiet a busy mind and soothe your fears. Do not stay in this position for too long, however, because it can become uncomfortable for your shoulders.

Exercise 6.11

Walking for stress relief and emotional release.

When something stressful is on your mind, go for a walk as soon as you can. While you are walking, hold the stressful memory in your mind and the feelings that go with it in your body. At the same time, your physical movement and awareness of your surroundings can keep your attention in the moment. Healing factor:

Being here and there at the same time

While walking, we can be present with both our physical environment and our memories, perhaps alternately. This dual awareness teaches the brain to toggle between the memory and the present moment, which is a sign of resilience as opposed to a fear of being consumed by stressful memories. This helps the brain to move through and integrate challenging emotions.

Why walking?
(Besides for good exercise)

This exercise was inspired by the story of how Francine Shapiro developed the EMDR (Eye Movement Desensitization and Reprocessing) technique because of a transformative walk. Following a stressful incident, Shapiro happened to walk through a local park. As she walked, she scanned her environment with her eyes while holding the stressful incident in mind. By the end of the walk, she noticed a significant feeling of emotional release.

This led Shapiro on a path of research and discovery into the experience. The result was EMDR, which is a treatment for the emotional impact of stress and trauma. EMDR centres around a concept called bilateral stimulation. This means that both sides of the brain are stimulated alternately for a period of time through a facilitating action. In therapy, the process can be facilitated by a client following the therapist's finger moving from side to side, or alternately tapping on their left and right legs, or tapping the left and right sides of the upper chest with arms crossed, while being guided to focus on and work through stressful memories.

Walking also has the effect of bilateral stimulation because the feet step and arms swing in rhythmic alternation. For stress and emotional relief, this is accompanied by a conscious intention to encourage a dual awareness of our internal, mental–emotional world and our external, physical environment.

When next you feel emotionally stressed, you can test this out for yourself by going for a conscious walk. A short walk on your closest nature trail might be all you need, or sometimes a longer walk or several walks might be necessary for bigger stressors or life-changing events. Walk at a pace that suits you. Allow for changes in your thoughts and feelings as you go along, as your mind opens to new ideas and perspectives. You might also find that past stresses come to mind, which might relate in some way to how you feel. Allow your mind to wander as it will. At the end of the walk, try recalling the original stress trigger and notice if your emotional reaction has changed in any way. Perhaps it has eased up, even if just a little. Another healing factor:

A feeling of moving forwards

The feeling of moving forwards while walking can be a metaphor for moving forward in our emotions and lives. This can feel empowering in contrast to feeling stuck. Walking is not a new idea for its potentially healing effects and ability to open our eyes to new insights and perspectives. There are many stories about people walking for days, weeks or months at a time to assist with grief and loss, or to inspire change, such as walking the famous Camino de Santiago trail as a personal pilgrimage.

Remember, if you have experienced trauma, it is not advisable to go it alone and try to walk through it. You may need professional help to support you through it.

chapter 7

Spotlight on depression

'People who have never dealt with depression think it's just being sad or being in a bad mood. That's not what depression is for me. It's falling into a state of greyness and numbness.' — **Dan Reynolds, Imagine Dragons**

This chapter's stress toolkit:

Exercise 7.1   Different ways to experience nervous system shut-down

 eeling sluggish, lethargic or unmotivated ? Has your energy been low? Or has an attitude of 'I can't be bothered' or 'I'm worthless' crept into certain aspects of your life? These might be signs of depression, which is more common and widespread than ever. Along with the pressures of living in our fast-paced, high-tech world, we've also had a global pandemic and the concomitant disruptions and adjustments to how we live our lives. All sorts of global stressors can confront us, such as war and crises like climate change. This is in addition to any issues on a personal level or in our relationships. It can feel exhausting at times.

Our suffering could also be existential; pain and loss are parts of life that cannot be avoided and might be difficult to work with. Our energy might come and go in waves, with times of high energy, inspiration and productivity followed by times of crashing into a creative funk. When this happens, how do we pick ourselves up and get going again?

The depression toolkit is designed to help. It contains various practical and creative options to experiment with towards discovering what works for you. This chapter provides an overview of the landscape of depression, from mild to severe, including when you should seek professional help.

Depression versus clinical depression

Depression can be a confusing topic because it is both a feeling (as in 'I feel depressed,' being synonymous for sad or unmotivated) and a diagnosable condition (such as major depressive disorder). Depression affects hundreds of millions of people globally. Some suffer from mild depression in response to perhaps a disappointment, recovery from illness or injury, or loss, such as of an important opportunity or a loved one. This is natural. As we move through these experiences, we can retain a belief that we will feel better eventually and that we can do something to help ourselves when we are ready.

When depression switches into a clinical disorder, experiences such as low energy and motivation; social isolation; negativity; sadness; dark mood; feeling empty, hopelessness or worthlessness; and loss of interest in once-enjoyable activities becomes chronic. Symptoms could also be masked by irritability, a state of confusion or inability to focus, or physical symptoms such as fatigue, headaches, digestive issues or significant change in weight.

Depressive disorders

According to the *Diagnostic and Statistical Manual of Mental Disorders*, for depression to be diagnosed as a disorder, symptoms need to persist for a period of time. For clinical or major depression, this is for most of the day for at least 2 weeks and in a way that significantly interferes with our ability to function day-to-day.

Depressive disorders include dysthymia, which is a mild, persistent depressive disorder, as well as postpartum depression and seasonal affective disorder. With depression of any kind, we can lose touch with the feeling that we can do something about it and be unwilling to receive support from others, perhaps believing that this too will be futile. It is common to feel really alone and lonely, even when we are in the company of others.

For the diagnosis and treatment of a depressive disorder, you should consult with a mental health professional.

Another possible cause for depression is grief. There is a difference between grief and depression. They do not necessarily go together, although they can. Grief is a natural process of working through the loss of a loved one, and takes time. It might involve being willing to feel our feelings as they rise and fall through our experience over time, and finding our way to move forwards in life. We may never fully 'recover' from grief like how we might hope to recover from depression. Grief is something that can redefine us and that we may need to integrate into our lives.

Gwen Flowers expresses this eloquently in a poem on grief:

And grief is not something you complete
But rather, you endure.
Grief is not a task to finish
And move on,
But an element of yourself –
An alteration of your being.
A new way of seeing.
A new definition of self.

Grief only turns to depression when we deny our feelings and remain numb to life. Perhaps we're denying ourselves a conscious process of grieving that might come and go in cycles. We may also be resisting the process of gradually integrating the loss into our lives over time.

At the root of depression is feeling stuck, together with an engulfing belief that how life is now, or how we feel now, is unchangeable. That nothing or no-one can really make a difference. Hopelessness, helplessness and lethargy can seep into every aspect of our lives, together with feelings of worthlessness and low self-esteem. Negative self-talk or negative thoughts can perpetuate these feelings, as can inactivity, isolation and possibly destructive, escapist behaviour.

Treating depression

Depression is treatable. If you suspect you might have a depressive disorder, seek professional evaluation and assistance to guide an appropriate treatment for you. The toolkits offered in this book can be helpful alongside professional consultation, potentially boosting a sense of empowerment and waking up interest in participating more fully with life.

So, how can you kindle hope that then goes on to start a meaningful change process? A helpful turning point can be as simple as realising that change is possible, which could apply to even a small change in our state of mind, our behaviour or how we feel in our bodies. Various tools in this depression toolkit can facilitate this.

Step-by-step, we can be led away from the patterns that sustained depression. Bear in mind that progress can feel circular – in that progress can be made, lost and made again. This is a natural part of growing more resilient.

Causes of depression

Causes can vary from trauma, family history, stress, illness or injury, to biochemical, neurological or genetic factors. The interaction of social, psychological and biological factors can lead to depression over time. Examples could be being bereaved, losing a job, feeling trapped in an unhealthy relationship, being injured or unwell, or experiencing a traumatic incident. Adverse life events may not cause depression, however; it has been found that good social support and a positive mindset can help us prevent or recover from depression more quickly, no matter what we might have gone through. Having practical tools to help us and some psycho-education can make a big difference too. Finding any way to believe that change is possible and holding on to even a glimmer of hope, from wherever it may come, is key to bouncing back and building stress resilience.

From our nervous system's perspective, any time we feel overwhelmed beyond our ability to fight back or flee, the next option is to shut down, go still or perhaps 'play dead', or try to hide to increase our chances of survival. When our bodies have turned to this strategy repeatedly, such as from repeated overwhelming or overpowering situations, our nervous systems become accustomed to shutting down. Shutting down can become a default stress response when we are faced with any hint of overwhelm, stress or challenge later in life. But even this habituated pattern can be worked through towards feeling more empowered.

Exercise 7.1

Different ways to experience nervous system shut-down

Here are some ways that nervous system shut-down can affect us. Not all lead to chronic depression and it can be helpful to become familiar with this range of possibilities to notice if we have this tendency (as opposed to high anxiety and mobilised stress response options like fight or flight).

1. Melancholy

When we think of depression, we usually think of the emotional or melancholic kind, linked to feeling sad, unmotivated, ashamed, unable to concentrate or apathetic. This possibly results from traumatic experience, significant loss or feeling disempowered. When we feel this way, it can be difficult to find the will to do what we might know is good for us, such as eating healthily, exercising, connecting with loved ones or achieving meaningful goals.

2. Mental alertness, physical shut-down

The nervous system can shut down in a non-emotional way, such as with screen-related apnoea. This can be caused by prolonged stillness from sitting in front of our computer screens in a focused way for work. While our minds remain alert and even creative, our breathing and metabolism can slow down significantly. The brain can interpret this motionlessness as a stress response similar to a dissociated freeze response, and it can take a while for our body and breathing to get going again once we move away from our screens.

3. Blank, numb, dissociated

When we become overwhelmed, we can shut down or withdraw. There may be too much going on all at once, too many thoughts swirling in our minds or situations that are beyond our ability to cope. The dorsal vagal pathway takes over, snapping us into a zoned-out state in which we dissociate from what is going on. This refers to the blank, numb or dissociated freeze response, as described in Chapter 2. Our sense of pain can be numbed too, thanks to the endorphins released naturally in these moments to increase our endurance of severe stress and our chances of survival. This can feel euphoric or floaty and even lead to out-of-body kinds of experiences. In extreme situations, we might actually faint, collapse or physically lose sensation in parts of our body.

4. Feeling sick to your stomach

When we get a big fright, hear shocking news or are suddenly confronted with a life-threatening situation, this can trigger another non-emotional nervous system shut-down. We can feel like we've been punched in the gut and feel sick to our stomach as our blood pressure dramatically drops. In extreme situations, we might actually throw up or pass out.

5. Alternating between acute sadness and numb, blank depression

When feeling depressed, especially following loss or trauma, it is common to have times when we feel the pain of our emotional wounds so acutely that we might sob uncontrollably or hurt intensely. A numb, blank state of depression can then set in, like an off switch triggered in the brain when our feelings are too much.

Although times of emotionality can form part of depression, when we do feel emotional, perhaps crying and hurting really badly, it is not shut-down response. Rather, it can be a sign of our nervous system coming back to life. From a psychological perspective, it can be helpful to feel our feelings as a necessary part of a recovery process, but in a guided or moderated way through professional support. Then we can be supported into a sense of moving forwards and through the pain, rather than getting stuck or lost in it.

The toolkit for depression

This toolkit is applicable no matter how our nervous system has shut down. Essentially, the task for all depression is to breathe new life into our nervous system. This can go on to energise us to actively seek out healing, meaning and fulfilment, and perhaps do some soul-searching. Rising out of depression can be a journey that takes time and draws on different interventions, such as those offered in this depression toolkit (chapters 7–11) and the shared toolkits for anxiety and depression (chapters 12–15).

From shut-down to revved-up before finding balance

When we begin to wake up from a collapse or blank, numb freeze response, it is possible to encounter all the potential energy of fight, flight or anxiety (sympathetic nervous system activation) that was shut down on freezing or collapsing. The anxiety toolkit in chapters 4–6 can be helpful here, as well as the summary chart of nine stress responses in Chapter 2, so you can gradually claim back your strength, confidence and ability to make a difference in your life.

Our bodies can move through some shivering, shaking and shuddering before settling back to feeling calm. This is how our nervous system releases pent-up energy. It is important to let this energy pass through us organically until it feels complete. This could be simply listening to how your body wants to go about it, perhaps encouraging the release of each shiver and shudder down and out through the arms or legs, or up and out through your head. You will know it is complete when your body feels more settled and perhaps a nice deep sigh of relief arrives too.

Being too hot or cold

Interestingly, the body experiences being too cold or too hot as stress responses. Being too cold can initiate shivering like the release of emotional energy or nervous system tension. No matter if our shivering is from cold or from emotional or shock release, we can follow what our bodies need. We can create warmth in other ways too, such as wearing warm clothing, rubbing our arms and moving into a warmer place.

In traditional Chinese medicine, there is a recommendation to always keep your lower back area warm, such as by wrapping a warm scarf around your waist if the weather is cold. You could also pause now and again throughout the day to rub your lower back. The kidneys are located in the lower back area, which are believed to relate to the emotion of fear. So keeping this area warm can help to keep fear, especially chronic fear, at bay.

Being too hot can lean us towards a collapsed stress response, because extreme heat can sap our energy. Helping our bodies cool down is a helpful solution towards restoring nervous system equilibrium. In other words, our bodies do not distinguish between emotional and environmental or physical causes of stress. The nervous system's response pathways are the same and can be dealt with in similar ways.

Depression in children and teenagers

Children and teenagers can show symptoms of depression. Depression can be triggered by, for example, physical illness, social dynamics at school, family dynamics at home or the loss of a loved one. It can be expressed in different ways, such as through angry outbursts, aggressive behaviour, or persistent low mood and sadness. This is different from short-lived emotional outbursts or sadness. As for adults, symptoms would need to persist for most of the day for a period of time.

There can be signs of depression that an adult can pick up on and ask about, such as withdrawal from friends or family, grades going down at school, loss of interest in once-enjoyed activities like dance or sport, or (with teenagers) use of alcohol or drugs. If depression is not remedied well when it first appears, usually with the support of a children's mental health specialist, it can lead to a long-term tendency towards depression, such as in the form of persistent or atypical depression, into adulthood.

Seeking the kinds of support to which a child or teenager might be open helps to get to the bottom of challenges or triggering situations and assist with problem-solving. School-based programs can also be helpful to raise awareness and provide support and resources. This is especially relevant for teenagers, whose hormonal changes can lead to confusing emotional highs, lows and reactivity regarding, for example, social dynamics and pressures to do well at school. Access to a school counsellor can also be helpful.

It is not something to feel ashamed of if a child or teenager needs professional support. Often, the skills learned in these early life contexts lead to valuable skills that can bolster mental health for life. As with the anxiety toolkit, teenagers can use the tools contained in the depression toolkit, allowing each individual to explore what might be most helpful to them. With younger children, a more imaginative, play-oriented approach might be needed. Working with a specialist in children's mental health or seeking out resources specifically for children is recommended.

Depression and suicidal thinking

Any time you think about taking your own life, or hear someone talking about it, it should be taken seriously. You should contact a trusted mental health professional or a facility specialising in suicide prevention or crisis intervention, such as calling your local suicide hotline.

If you find yourself in a position where someone shares with you that they have suicidal thoughts, talk to them about it and find out how seriously they have considered it, such as if they have a specific plan to take their life or have tried to do so before. Once you have allowed for the expression of feelings, you can encourage an exploration of alternative options for solving their problems. It is important to realise that death is final, but crises can be temporary and solvable.

chapter 8

Depression toolkit: Mind

'Do not let what you cannot do interfere with what you can do.' — **John Wooden**

This chapter's stress toolkit:

Exercise 8.1 Identify common themes of the depressed mind

Exercise 8.2 Notice the negative

Exercise 8.3 Reality test and reframe the negative

Exercise 8.4 Pump up the positive

Exercise 8.5 Some journaling ideas helpful with depression

ur thoughts can play a big part in keeping depression in place. As with anxiety, there is negative self-talk, although for depression the themes might differ. Anxiety can feel more like a mental flight into worst-case scenarios we might desperately want to avoid, and that might also be accompanied by a harsh inner critic. Depression can feel more like dropping into a deep, dark underworld, weighed down by debilitating thoughts and beliefs about life and ourselves. It can be different for different people, such as feeling like withdrawing, becoming invisible, spacing out or playing dead. Or it can hurt and cut us up inside. When the emotional pain rises to the surface, it can feel unbearable or overwhelming. At some point, an internal trip-switch inside the brain and nervous system kicks in to dull or shut down our ability to experience pain. Biologically, this is designed to help us endure hardship by going numb to it.

This chapter targets depression at the mental level, identifying common themes of the depressed mind and offering tools that include noting the negative, reality testing and reframing our thoughts, as well as pumping up the positives to counterbalance negativity. The practices in the shared depression and anxiety toolkits in chapters 12–15 can also intercept negative thinking, spark inspiration and open our minds to support and guide our progress. Together, this range of tools can gently coax or rigorously shake up rigid thinking patterns that might not serve us well, and promote a more nourishing and uplifting experience of life.

You are invited to treat these toolkits as a journey of exploration. Not all techniques are for everyone. Follow what resonates with you. If something kindles your curiosity, go there. If something raises resistance inside you, honour that too and find a starting point that feels more inviting. It is a delicate task to lure a spirit back into the body and into being willing to engage more fully with life. Be gentle and kind with yourself.

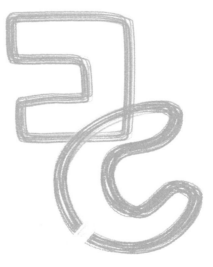

Exercise 8.1

Identify common themes of the depressed mind

What does your mind come up with? As you read through the various options, consider if any are familiar to you. You might also notice other ways that your mind brings you down or might keep you feeling flat that you could add to this list.

1. 'I don't feel like it.' – Low motivation

Anything outside of our comfort zone might feel like too much effort.

2. 'It is like this.' – Rigid, fixed thinking patterns

We base these on assumptions and finite conclusions, usually around the themes of worthlessness and helplessness. This rigid thinking can focus on loss of trust in ourselves, our abilities, others or the world. We can think shameful, belittling beliefs about ourselves, like we are flawed and inadequate. All-or-nothing and black-and-white thinking can play a part here too, such as believing we are a failure or success with nothing in between.

3. 'It is always going to be this way.' – Global statements

We can make sweeping generalisations about ourselves, which are usually degrading and can include words such as always, all, forever, never and nobody. For example, 'Everyone hates me'; 'I am a terrible person' or a failure, not worthy or not loveable; 'Nothing is ever going to change and nobody can do anything to help'; 'Horrible things always happen to me'; 'Nobody ever understands me'; 'There is something wrong with me' or 'I am useless'. These thoughts come from a tendency to apply difficulties in the past to how things will turn out in the future, which we cannot really know.

4. 'I'm never going to match up.' – Negative comparisons and assumptions

This is when we belittle ourselves, our abilities or our self-worth. We might also assume that others think or speak badly of us, without actually knowing if this is true.

5. 'I should be doing something else.' – Shoulds and ought tos

These focus on what we believe we are not doing or not able to do, as opposed to focusing on what we can do or are already doing. If we focus on what we should or ought to be doing, or how we should or ought to be different, it can lead to a gap between ourselves and who we believe we 'should' be, which can feed into depression.

6. 'This is the worst thing ever and it's going to last forever.' – Catastrophising

Especially when intense sadness, anger or pain rises to the surface, it can feel intensely overwhelming. We might fear that it is going to last forever and never subside. Our minds can spin with worst-case scenarios that intensify fear and pain. Destructive behaviour might follow, like wanting to hurt ourselves to try to release the pain, or escape through a vice of choice, or oversleep to tune out of it.

7. 'I can't think of anything at all.' – Blankness, emptiness, mental fog

There might be brain fog, complete dissociation or spaciness, together with feeling nothing at all. This can feel relieving, like going on a mental vacation and tuning out of our problems. But it does not help to solve our problems, which will still be there when we tune in again. Under extreme stress, tuning out can be a life saver to help endure hardship. But at some point, we have to return to the present moment to address what we need to. The breathing and body-based toolkits in chapters 9–11 can be particularly helpful to address this kind of experience.

4 ways to combat negativity

The following tools are designed to facilitate a shift from a fixed or rigid mindset to one of possibility, creativity and a willingness to learn and grow from experience. In the process, we can come to befriend our thinking mind, as opposed to fighting or fearing it.

The tools include:

- Exercise 8.2 Notice the negative
- Exercise 8.3 Reality test and reframe the negative
- Exercise 8.4 Pump up the positive
- Exercise 8.5 Some journaling ideas helpful with depression

It can be helpful to keep a journal as you begin to explore your thoughts. In this way, you have a place to gather, reflect on, and look back on themes and patterns of thinking. You could also use this journal to practise skills, such as reality testing and reframing negatives as positives, to encourage new lines of thought. You might appreciate writing in your journal to clear your mind at the end of each day, or starting your day in a thought-provoking way by gathering your thoughts and perhaps setting intentions. Explore what works best for you.

Exercise 8.2

Notice the negative

Become your own detective on the lookout for negative thoughts. Here is an opportunity to focus on the kinds of thoughts your mind comes up with. Do your thoughts catastrophise or overgeneralise? Does a loud inner critic put you down or have beliefs about the world that hold you back? Do you assume that others speak or think badly of you? Carrying a pen and notebook with you can be helpful to spot negativity. You can quickly jot things down and pick up on thought themes. Later, you can write these into a journal dedicated to this process, if you choose to keep one.

Exercise 8.3

Reality test and reframe the negative

Realising that your thoughts are not always facts can be liberating. It is true that bad things can happen and that you can receive so-called negative feedback from others. But much of the time, the reality is not as bad as your thoughts make it out to be. Reality testing invites an investigation of assumptions and conclusions to shake them up a little and open the possibility of seeing situations differently. Reframing is then a process of considering your thoughts in a different light, which might build rather than break your confidence and sense of worth. Both reality testing and reframing can counteract rigid thinking and create more flexibility in how we habitually think.

1. Turn a statement into a question.

If you catch a statement like 'I'm not good enough', try turning it into a question, such as: 'Am I not good enough?' Then allow your mind to come up with its own responses. If your mind persists with negativity, you might keep asking questions like 'Am I really not good enough? How do I know that for sure?' Another example is 'They think I am stupid'. You might change that to 'Do they think I am stupid? How do I know that for sure?' Talking this through with someone who cares can also be helpful.

2. Consider, is it true? Are you sure? What evidence do you have?

You ask questions directed at your negativity or your inner critic, such as 'Who actually said it?' 'How many people have said that to you?' 'How often have you heard it?' Or any other way you might test the validity of your thoughts and beliefs.

3. Look for exceptions.

When depressed, we can lose the ability and desire to recognise the positives. Deliberately looking for exceptions can remind us of times when we might not feel quite so depressed. Then we can go on to be curious about what we do that feels nourishing and supportive, so we can do more of it to lift our mood. To help, you might consider which people treat you differently, perhaps like you matter and are important in some way. Are there certain situations – like when you are at home, at work or school, or spending time with friends – when you feel differently from now? You might ask yourself, 'Do I really feel depressed every minute of every day, or are there times when my mood is not so low?'

4. Replace a negative thought with a more helpful one.

You could reframe a thought like 'This will never work' to something like 'What are some things I can try now?' Or change 'I am useless' to 'I might have made a mistake, but how can I learn from it and carry on?' This shifts your focus away from problems being permanent and conclusions about ourselves being finite, into an attitude of learning and growth. Or you could ask yourself, 'If this thought was not here, what else would be here instead?' This can loosen up fixed lines of thinking and open up creativity (even if we do pick another negative, maybe we can laugh about it rather than feeling as troubled by it).

Like with all-or-nothing or black-and-white thinking, it can be a pitfall to replace a finite negative like 'I am a failure' with a finite positive like 'I am a success'. Our minds can quickly turn this back into 'I am a failure' when we don't achieve success or meet setbacks. In this case, it can be more helpful to acknowledge your effort rather than a failure or success. Try redirecting your thinking to something like 'I am doing my best' and consider how you can learn and grow through the experience. Asking a friend to ask you these questions can also be helpful to encourage perseverance.

5. Be prepared that positive thinking can trigger negativity.

Opening to more positivity can be unfamiliar and scary. It can even trigger a barrage of negative thoughts, rising up like an army to defend old familiar ways. Whenever emotions rise up and feel intense, we can be helped by a soothing strategy from the body toolkit for depression (see Chapter 10), such as placing a hand on the centre of your chest and breathing mindfully through your feelings. It can take time for old habits to shift and for trust to build in new ways of thinking.

6. Label as 'thought' or 'negative thought'.

This mindfulness practice offers a way to detach from thinking in general to loosen up emotional involvement in our thoughts. It involves labelling thoughts simply as 'thought' or 'negative thought'. Some find it liberating right away, while others might prefer it after graduating with sufficient awareness of negative thought themes. You might start by trying it out as a meditation practice for a minute or two, setting aside a few minutes once a day for a week to observe the contents of your mind. Each time a thought arises, positive or negative, you simply label it as a thought then wait to see what comes next.

Images often used in teaching mindfulness can be helpful here; for example, seeing thoughts as clouds passing through the clear blue sky of consciousness. Rather than jumping aboard a passing cloud, you could simply notice it passing by while being curious about the stillness of the sky between your cloudy thoughts.

Exercise 8.4

Pump up the positive

'Hope is curiosity writ large. [It is a] willingness to cultivate within yourself whatever kindles light and to shine that light into the darkest places.' — **Edith Eger**, *The Gift*

With depression, it is possible to lose sight of moments of positivity throughout the day. This does not mean that they are not there. Moments of lightness, awe or beauty might lift our spirits spontaneously, such as from a happy memory, a sight or a smile, but then quickly slide out of awareness again. How can we pay more attention to and enhance these moments to counteract depression? That is what this section is about.

When we feel uplifted, it feeds vital nourishment to our wholesome, restorative nervous system (the ventral vagus nerve pathway). The more we can notice moments of upliftment and enhance the experience by staying with the feelings for a bit longer, the more receptive our nervous system can become to positivity. This can serve as a buffer against negativity and depression. Some days might be easier and other days more difficult, but perseverance will pay off. Here are some ways to pay more attention to the positives.

1. Pay more attention to what lifts your spirits.

For a few days in a row, make a point to intentionally notice what lights you up, from the tiniest things such as the smile of a stranger, to the biggest such as something wonderful happening in your life. The more you practise, the easier it will become to tell the difference between what drags you down and lifts you up. You might naturally find yourself moving towards what brings you joy and makes you feel more alive. In the words of the visionary Howard Thurman, 'Don't ask yourself what the world needs, ask yourself what makes you come alive, and go do that, because what the world needs is people who have come alive.'

2. Keep a gratitude journal.

Another way to pay more attention to the positives is to keep a gratitude journal. This is a daily invitation to reflect back your day for a period of time, and identify at least three things that genuinely lifted your spirits, even if just a little bit. It could be the traffic that flowed more smoothly than usual, a story you heard on the radio, a memory that surfaced, a beautiful flower, or simple gratitude for having a roof over your head or for the sun shining. There is no limit to what these experiences can entail, only that they lift your spirits and spark some gratitude.

3. Name 100 things that lift your spirits (or used to).

This is a recommendation from psychologist Dr Shelly Harrell. Taking all the time that you need, months if need be, come up with a list of 100 things that you like or used to like, even if you can't feel it now. This could be the smallest things, such as your favourite colours or artworks, spending time in nature, listening to particular music, playing certain games, people you like, sports, dance, a talent you might have lost touch with, your favourite places to go and your favourite foods to eat.

Completing this long list of 100 things you like, or once liked, can trick your brain into realising that there is a lot you do like in life. In turn, this can prompt a more positive outlook and an interest in moving towards these kinds of activities.

Exercise 8.5

Some journaling ideas helpful with depression

If journaling is something that works for you, here are some ideas to add to your journaling practice. These suggestions can complement the writing ideas in the anxiety toolkit and can support you in turning around mental patterns of depression.

Link thoughts, feelings and actions or behaviour.

Seeing the connections between thoughts, feelings and behaviours can help you to realise you can be an active player in how you feel by choosing to act differently or exploring new lines of thinking, such as suggested earlier in this chapter.

- Name and write some details about the feelings that go with your thoughts. You might consider where in your body you feel them. Then consider the activities or behaviours that might emanate from these thoughts and feelings.

- Reflect on times, perhaps during the day or the previous week, when you did not feel as depressed. Note the kinds of activities you were involved in at the time, which might have led you to feeling better, as well as how you felt at the time and the kinds of thoughts with you.

- List activities that lift your mood. After some time reflecting in this way, you might be able to list the kinds of activities and accompanying thoughts that lift your mood versus those that depress you.

Pay attention to emotional ups and downs.

- For journaling at the end of the day, you could reflect back on your day and write about your emotional ups and downs. This can help you see them more clearly; especially with depression, this can be a helpful skill. With depression, we can lose sight of the fact that there are ups and downs. Journaling can have an added benefit of stimulating memory, which can counteract the gaps in memory or poor memory that can come with depression.

○ You can link this to the previous journaling exercise by paying attention to the kinds of activities that lift your mood, such as being productive at work, speaking with a particular person, spending time with a pet or exercising. This adds to your awareness of which activities support your upliftment. The sooner you can realise that you can make a difference to how you feel, to your life and perhaps even to our world, the better for your depression recovery.

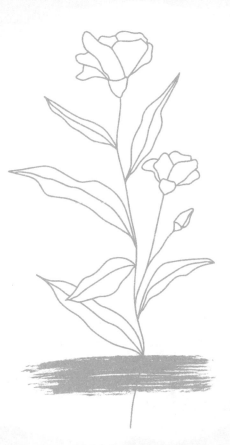

chapter 9

Depression toolkit:
Breathing

'Your body is your first home. Breathing
in, I arrive in my body. Breathing
out, I am home.' — **Thich Nhat Hanh**

This chapter's stress toolkit:

Exercise 9.1   Observe natural breathing for 1–5 minutes

Exercise 9.2   Breathing through your heart

Exercise 9.3   Breathing while thinking, breathing while feeling

Exercise 9.4   Gently revitalising whole-body breathing practice

Exercise 9.5   A breathing practice for discovering your
inner alchemist

Exercise 9.6   Tips to restore vitality after spending time focused
on a screen

reathing is a wonderful way to energise your nervous system and inspire your mind. Whereas anxiety requires that we learn to let go and exhale more fully, depression can require us to inhale more fully. Inhaling can take courage because it can feel like allowing ourselves to grow bigger and take up more space in ourselves and our lives. For this reason, when we are depressed, getting started with the first tiny mindful inhalations can be a challenge as there might be resistance to opening up. Fears, unresolved grief or trauma and numbness can get in the way of our willingness to try. You are invited to adopt an attitude of experimentation and curiosity, knowing that the breathing practices in this chapter are really gentle to get you started.

Breathing new life into yourself

A common theme for the breathing practices for working for depression is breathing new life into yourself. To facilitate this, the breathing practices are designed to be gentle and subtly energising for your mind and body. There are six breathing practices on offer here for your experimentation at different times and in no particular order. As you go along, you might find that you enjoy a particular one, which you can then allocate as your go-to breathing intervention possibly for years to come.

An excellent starting point is the simple practice of slow breathing, also known as resonance frequency breathing, introduced in Exercise 5.5 of the anxiety toolkit. It is equally applicable to working with depression and can be subtly energising. It involves taking five slow breaths to a mental count of five on inhalation and five on exhalation. Breathing is recommended to be as light as a feather (so a feather under your nose would barely move) and breathing all through your nose if you can. The gentleness of this practice can be just what is needed to wake you up to feeling a little better. You can use it any time when feeling down.

Exercise 9.1

Observe natural breathing for 1–5 minutes

1. Find a quiet moment to pay attention to your breathing.

Make yourself comfortable in an upright seated position, propped up by cushions if you need to. Set a timer so you can immerse in the experience with your eyes closed (if this is comfortable for you to do).

2. Start noticing your breath for a few moments.

See how your breath comes and goes naturally through your nose and lungs (if your nose is blocked, focus on the flow of breath through your mouth). Perhaps your breath is deep and long, or shallow and short.

3. Observe your breathing in different ways.

Pay attention to the temperature of the air as it enters and leaves your nose, noticing how your in-breath is cooler and out-breath is warmer because your nasal passages are warming and humidifying the air. See how far your inhalation is drawn into your body and how far out it reaches on exhalation. Become curious about which parts of your chest or belly are involved in your breathing. Is your breathing limited to high up in your chest, or does your belly also move with each breath? This might change as you bring awareness to it and perhaps are curious to explore deeper breathing.

4. Any time you might need it, ground and refocus.

If at any point you feel light-headed, slow your breathing down and make it lighter, or pause for a few moments and place a hand on top of your head for some grounding. As you continue to observe your natural breath, you might catch your mind wandering. This is natural. Kindly and simply return your focus to your breathing. In itself, this returning to where you choose to focus attention will grow your mental muscle for presence.

With practice, you can improve this ability to direct and hold your attention where you choose, such as away from past-based rumination or future-based worry and into the clearer light of the present moment.

Exercise 9.2

Breathing through your heart

Here is a short process for shifting gears away from negativity or numbness into heart-based feelings such as compassion, kindness and love. You can use this practice anytime, such as first thing in the morning to set a heartfelt tone for the day, or last thing at night before sleep to infuse your mind and any memories from the day with some loving-kindness.

1. Bring your awareness into your heart area.

You can imagine entering a lift in your mind and travelling down to your heart. Or you can place a hand over your heart or centre of your chest for a few moments to invite your awareness there. Placing a small smile on your face can also be helpful, possibly imagining a warm 'hello' to your heart.

2. Feel your breathing through your heart.

Imagine that your breathing flows smoothly in and out through your heart or centre of your chest. Gradually slow down your breathing to wake up your relaxation response more strongly, perhaps until your breathing is a mental count of about four to six on each in-breath and the same on the out-breath. Breathe only through your nose if you can.

3. Amplify the experience.

Call to mind someone you love unconditionally or something that easily warms your heart, such as a special person, pet or your favourite place. Hold this in your mind as you continue to breathe through your heart.

4. Continue for as long as you wish.

Even three to five slow breaths, or continuing for a minute or two, can shift your mood towards more kindness and caring. If your emotions open up and tears come, know that these tears are cleansing, helping to wash away pain with time. Stay with the experience for as long as you wish.

Note: This heart-focused breathing exercise is inspired by the Heartmath Institute, which has spent decades researching the measurable effects of heartfelt living on personal, interpersonal and global levels. The benefits are clear and numerous. They stem from accessing the wholesome, nourishing ventral vagus nerve pathway of the parasympathetic nervous system, which is the source of our health, growth and restoration physically, mentally and emotionally.

Exercise 9.3

Breathing while thinking, breathing while feeling

This can be an interesting challenge to experiment with. Next time you catch yourself thinking or feeling emotional in some way, ask yourself 'Am I breathing?' If not, or if you are barely breathing, invite yourself to continue with your thoughts and feelings, but while breathing naturally and steadily. How does this influence you?

Most of us fall prey to holding our breath, or breathing shallowly, while lost in thought and feelings. Becoming conscious of our breathing, and perhaps slowing down breathing, can help slow down our thinking and ease the intensity of our feelings. The increase in relaxation and better oxygenation of body and brain can help us think more clearly and respond from a more conscious place.

Exercise 9.4

Gently revitalising whole-body breathing practice

This breathing practice can be carried out in 5 minutes in a break in your day, or you can expand it into a longer practice by increasing the number of breaths you take at the different stages of the process and by extending the time you spend afterwards soaking up the mindful stillness that follows. Take care to breathe naturally or lighter and slower than usual for the soothing effect. This practice can have a subtly energising effect, so it might not be helpful when trying to fall asleep at night, although some do find it helpful then.

1. Find a comfortable spot.

Start in a comfortable sitting or lying position. If you are sitting, prop yourself up comfortably.

2. Breathe into your head.

Take three slow and even breaths as if your whole head, including your face, breathes with you, gently filling and emptying with each breath.

3. Breathe with your whole chest.

Take three slow and even breaths as if your whole chest breathes with you. You might explore expanding your chest in all directions with each inhalation – forwards, backwards and sideways – to more fully allow your breath to penetrate and open this area. Then you can explore emptying your chest area more fully on each exhalation.

4. Breathe with your whole torso.

For three breaths, include your whole torso as if your whole torso area, between the hips and shoulders, fills and empties with each inhalation and exhalation.

5. Breathe with your legs and arms.

For three breaths, imagine as if your legs and arms breathe along with each inhalation and exhalation, filling and emptying and feeling more alive.

6. Breathe with your whole body.

Take three breaths with your body as a whole, as if your whole body gently breathes with each inhalation and exhalation, filling, emptying and feeling alive.

7. Relax, let go.

Spend a few moments letting go of any intentional breathing and soaking up how you feel after this practice. When we slow down and embody our breathing, it can improve blood circulation and oxygen delivery to our cells for a subtle energy boost, which can support both physical and mental health.

Exercise 9.5

A breathing practice for discovering your inner alchemist

This is a practice combining conscious breathing and colour visualisation. It can build a quality of inner, heartfelt strength. It can also potentially reduce feelings of overwhelm by waking up the transformative power inside ourselves to turn negativity and suffering into light and well-wishes.

The practice is inspired by an ancient Tibetan mindfulness practice, called Tonglen, that draws on breathing coordinated with an intention to give and receive in a supportive way. It aims to cultivate qualities such as compassion, loving-kindness and altruism, which can be a helpful in working with depression.

Breathing

Use natural or slowed-down (lengthened) breathing throughout this exercise, with equal lengths of inhalation and exhalation.

Visualisation

Visualise breathing in darkness, perhaps as black or grey smoke or negativity in some form. Then visualise breathing out light, perhaps as white or golden light or any shade that feels good. You might imagine you are an alchemist, who can turn lead into gold, or negativity into light. You might imagine breathing in depression, guilt, shame, anxiety or whatever. Then breathe out qualities such as love and kindness with the light. You might conceive of these qualities originating from some place deep inside you, perhaps your heart, where light can be made.

Each time you breathe out, let your breath meander out into the space around you. If your imagination is open to it, you might imagine your exhalations filling the space around you, possibly reaching further outwards into the greater world or being directed to the image of a person you know who may need it.

Here are some visualisation options to help you connect with light by drawing on nature or the universe at the transformative moment at the end of inhalation:

- Think of the different universal sources of light, including the sun, moon and stars, that can help you switch on light inside yourself. Choose the kind of light that feels good and include it in your visualisation to help you connect with light.

- Visualise the bright sun appearing and allow it to fill you with its golden warmth and glow, which you breathe out. Or perhaps the silvery light of the bright full moon speaks to you, piercing the darkness with its silvery emanations that you release with your out-breath.

- Imagine your body breathing in darkness like the night sky, then at the internal turning point, your whole body fills with stars and you breathe out their rainbow sparkle.

Repeat for 2–5 minutes

Experiment with expanding this into a 10–15 minute meditation practice. Each time you breathe in, allow negativity or darkness to ride your in-breath, and positivity and light to ride your out-breath. You might slow down your breathing to increase the relaxation effect and avoid hyperventilation, which can come from trying too hard or being too vigorous with breathing.

Note that this practice can be difficult at first. Keep in mind that it does get easier with practice. At first, an intention might simply be to pierce a dark mood with even the tiniest window of light to show you it might be possible. From there, if the practice resonates with you, you can expand the visualisation and grow your relationship with your ability to generate light, opening up to the possibility of being a source of light for yourself and the world in your unique way.

Expand on the practice

This practice has traditionally been used to transform the suffering of others, such as imagining breathing in the suffering or pain of someone you know, or whole communities, and breathing out healing, soothing light directed to your mental image of them. Along with the light, you can add a wish to ease their suffering. Tonglen meditation is believed to have been initiated in the 11th century as a distance healing technique during a leprosy crisis.

You can also personalise the practice if you have been feeling down by imagining yourself as hunched over and small somewhere in front of you. Then a bigger part of yourself carries out this practice, directing light and an intention for healing or easing suffering to your more vulnerable self. Imagine breathing in that smaller person's hurt, negativity or shame in the form of darkness or black smoke. Now breathe out light, love and kindness towards them, perhaps as smoky peachy pinks and yellows, or as a quality of light you can connect with, to surround them.

Play with these ideas if they interest you. There are many studies showing the effectiveness of this kind of practice for improving mood and honing our ability to be compassionate. This can benefit us and others whose lives we touch.

Exercise 9.6

Tips to restore vitality after spending time focused on a screen

As mentioned in the breathing toolkit for anxiety in Chapter 5, screen or email apnoea involves a tendency to hold our breath or barely breathe for extended periods of time while sitting still in front of a computer and working in a focused way.

This stillness or immobilisation with intense focus can be interpreted by the brain as stress in the form of a dissociated freeze response. At those times, we can feel disconnected from our emotions and our environment. This sense of disconnection can bear some resemblance to the dissociation or emotional disconnection that depression can bring.

Here are some ways to restore vitality after a period of screen-based dissociation:

1. Catch then reboot your breathing.

To start with, notice if you are breathing or holding your breath while focusing on a screen. This often goes along with body tension, such as in your back or neck and perhaps your arms. You might create a reminder to encourage catching this, such as by placing a note to yourself somewhere around your workspace. This could be a screen saver to remind you to breathe, or a post-it note with 'Are you breathing?' written on it and placed where you can easily see it.

A beautiful picture or an oil burner with a lovely scent, or some plants or flowers in your workspace can also inspire you to breathe when you remember to admire them now and again. Experiment with what works for you. Once you reboot your breathing, adjust your posture to be comfortably upright before resuming your focused work.

2. Gradually encourage your breathing down to the level of your diaphragm.

Tension, especially in the upper body or throat, can make it more difficult to resume breathing more deeply. It might take some encouragement to ease up tense areas to allow your breath to flow again. If this is the case, start by exploring where you are with two or three natural breaths into your throat or wherever your breath feels caught. Gently encourage the area to relax and open. Then take two or three more gentle breaths into an area below that, such as your upper chest.

Gradually progress in this way, easing your breath lower in your body until your diaphragm or belly can move with your breathing. Your diaphragm, which is the muscle separating chest from abdomen, is your ideal breathing muscle. Enjoy two or three more breaths with awareness of your whole body breathing along with you, which can boost a sense of vitality.

3. Deepen your breathing and extend exhalation.

Take at least three breaths (all through the nose if you can) where your exhalation is longer than your inhalation. You might follow the 4–6 ratio. Breathe in for a slow count of four, then breathe out for a count of six or more if you can.

Consciously exhaling activates the calming branch of our parasympathetic nervous system, as opposed to the dull, numbing dorsal vagal branch responsible for the dissociated freeze response. This can help your body and brain to wake up and feel more refreshed.

4. Use breath-holding consciously.

Box breathing is a way to increase the oxygenation of your body and brain and refresh your energy. This technique was introduced in Exercise 5.6 of the breathing toolkit for anxiety (Chapter 5). A summary is to breathe in for a slow count of four, hold your breath at the top of your inhalation for the count of four, exhale for the count of four and finally hold your breath at the end of your exhalation for the count of four. This is one round of box breathing.

Repeat three times (or more if you like), breathing all through your nose if you can or in through your nose and out through your mouth for stronger stress relief.

5. Get moving.

Whether you get up to stretch and walk about, or sit on a gym ball and move your hips around the ball, taking a break at regular intervals can help you stay focused, helping blood flow through your body and your breathing to normalise.

Tim Walker, an American teacher who is based in Finland, has written about how some schools in Finland have adopted a practice of students taking active breaks every 45 minutes for 15 minutes because of the effective results. It is up to you whether to adopt such a regular practice or simply to take better care in actively loosening up your body and breathing when you take a break from your screen-based work.

Keeping up with a regular exercise routine at a time of day that works for you is also recommended to counteract screen apnoea, as well as taking any opportunity to put on music and dance to keep your posture loose and spirits uplifted.

chapter 10

Depression toolkit: Body

'If you keep your heart open through everything, your pain can become your greatest ally in your life's search for love and wisdom.' — **Rumi (13th century Sufi poet)**

This chapter's stress toolkit:

Exercise 10.1 Postural shift to take a stand in yourself, for yourself or for what you believe in

Exercise 10.2 'SEW' yourself back together again – a self-soothing compassion practice for difficult emotions

Exercise 10.3 Quiet your mind, soothe your emotions and feel more present with self-supportive touch

hile anxiety needs calming down, depression needs energising and upliftment. Finding the will, motivation and strength to do so can be challenging. But there are creative ways to go about it. The exercises in this chapter focus on drawing on the body as a resource. From a physical point of view, getting moving and breathing more fully is key to being able to engage more fully with life. Keep up with your preferred exercise program, such as running, walking, yoga, qigong, swimming, going to the gym, dancing, or whatever you prefer.

Much research backs the benefits of physical exercise for counteracting symptoms of depression and uplifting our spirits.

This chapter looks at ways to draw on our bodies beyond what our exercise programs can provide to support healing and personal growth. It contains short practices you can use on-the-spot to boost inner strength and lift your spirits. The more often we take mini breaks throughout the day to use practices like these, the more we can strengthen our self-worth and tone our wholesome ventral vagal nervous system to counteract symptoms of depression. Even 30 seconds of one of these interventions, practised once or twice a day for a few consecutive days, can start to rewire your brain towards lasting positive change.

As with all the toolkits of this book, we suggest reading the chapter and skimming through the exercises. Then try out what might pique your curiosity, knowing you can return to try out other techniques at other times.

Short practices for boosting inner strength and lifting your spirits

Exercise 10.1

Postural shift to take a stand in yourself, for yourself or for what you believe in

This exercise helps to boost strength, courage and determination in a grounded way that also makes space for tenderness. Use it whenever you feel you need it, such as just before an important meeting. Or perhaps when your inner critic or negativity gets too loud and you wish to take a stand against it, and steer your thinking in more helpful directions. The practice involves a three-point check accompanied by a short breathing practice for consolidating the outcome. You can carry it out in a couple of minutes or practise it for longer if you like.

The three-point check

1. Ground through your feet.

If you are standing, stand evenly on both feet and feel the pull of gravity from your hips down your legs and into the ground through your feet. Stand with weight evenly distributed on the undersides of your feet (under the balls of your feet, toes and heels, even if you are wearing shoes). If you are sitting, ground through your feet and seat, placing both feet evenly on the ground and centring your weight over your hips in your sitting position.

2. Strong back

To the best of your ability and without straining, lengthen your back so your spine might feel a two-way pull, upwards to the sky through your head and downwards to the ground through your tailbone. Feel the strength of your uprightness rising up your back to hold you tall and connect you with qualities such as determination, courage and focus.

3. Soft front

While maintaining your sense of strength through uprightness in your back, allow your heart to open. You might place a hand on the centre of your chest or rub this area for some soothing. We need our strength but we also need tenderness, otherwise too much tension can accumulate and tire us. Where might you need this tenderness in your life? Perhaps towards yourself or someone you love who needs some care. Or perhaps you might need to forgive yourself for something you had no control over. Or maybe you need some strength to admit you made a mistake and some tenderness to ask for forgiveness.

Three circular breaths

If you just have a moment, adjusting your posture with the three-point check can sometimes do the trick on its own. If you have a few moments more, add three conscious breaths to further energise your posture.

- Take three long, slow breaths while imagining your breath moving up your back on inhalation and down your front on exhalation. Each time you breathe in, you might imagine the air rising up your spine to energise your uprightness before circling overhead. Then imagine the air descending down the front of your body as you breathe out, releasing into qualities such as softness and surrender. The air circles at the base of your spine before rising up your back again with your next inhalation.

- Continue to circle your breath in this way three to nine times then breathe naturally and pause for a few moments to soak up how you feel. Reflect on what piece of advice you can give yourself from this headspace, or what you wish to take a heartfelt stand for today.

Microcosmic orbit

This breathing practice is inspired by an ancient Taoist energy cultivation technique called the microcosmic orbit. It is used to energise a central, internal energy pathway in the body known as the 'governing vessel' considered central to health and vitality. The breathing practice follows an energetic circular pathway from the pelvic floor, running upwards along the spine to the crown of the head before circling down the front of the body over the face, throat, chest, stomach and returning to the pelvic floor. It can bring a sense of balance to body and mind because of the constant cycling between upward-moving, outgoing yang energy and downward-moving, introspective yin energy.

Life is a dynamic balance between needing to be strong and active, and needing to soften and surrender into meaningful connection with others and for rest and restoration. This breathing practice can remind us of those contrasting qualities and hone our ability to enter into each of them, perhaps more consciously or in a more balanced way.

We can also use this practice to strengthen our relationship with ourselves. Circling the energy up and down our bodies can remind us to transition more fluidly between the different aspects of ourselves. If our minds are overactive, it can remind us to tune into our hearts and descend into our instinctive gut feelings for the perspective they can bring, then return when we are ready up to the wisdom of our minds.

Exercise 10.2

SEW yourself back together again – a self-soothing compassion practice for difficult emotions

Being numb to emotional pain, as can happen with depression, can bring welcome relief. Unfortunately, it does not solve our problems but simply delays our need to face them, and possibly causes further problems if we have turned to addictive behaviours to sustain our numbness. At other times, feelings might rise to the surface and be intense and difficult to sit with.

This exercise offers a way to soothe our emotions on-the-spot and lets us connect with ourselves in a supportive way. It can boost emotional resilience, lessen feelings of being overwhelmed and grow our tolerance for our emotions. As a result, we may no longer need to go numb to our feelings.

Compassion-based mindfulness

This exercise draws on research-backed methods from compassion-based mindfulness practice, such as introduced by Kristin Neff and Christopher Germer as well as research by Richard Davidson. Certain components need to be present to maximise the potential for self-compassion to build emotional resilience and boost inner strength in a heartfelt way.

The first component is mindfulness, specifically building the mindful ability to hold our awareness on our feelings in a way that is not overwhelming.

The second component is an attitude of kindness and caring towards ourselves and others. Towards ourselves, it can counteract self-criticism or self-judgment. Some of us might find it easier to foster this attitude towards others so the one can feed the other.

The third component involves expanding awareness to the level of common or shared humanity so we realise that we are not alone in our experience – many others struggle too, perhaps in similar ways. This can counteract a sense of isolation or feeling all alone in what we are going through, which can be common with depression.

The acronym 'SEW' guides you in a self-compassion experience that you can use whenever you feel emotional or are having a hard time.

- **S – 'soothe and soften'** to build mindfulness of our feelings in a way that reduces the likelihood of feeling overwhelmed.
- **E – 'enquire'** into what is needed, which is a gesture of loving-kindness and caring towards ourselves.
- **W – 'wish well'** as a gesture of loving-kindness towards ourselves and others.

Once you know the stages, you can carry out this practice in just a minute or two. You might imagine SEW-ing yourself back together emotionally towards feeling more contained. This practice can be useful at times when emotions feel intense, such as when you might be hurting or feeling scared. Or perhaps you have been on the receiving end of negativity, criticism or self-criticism, which has sent you into a spin. You can also use it when you feel numb as a gentle way to open up to feeling again.

The SEW practice

Soothe and soften

1. When you notice you are hurting or struggling in some emotional way, perhaps sadness or guilt or shame has visited you, first place a hand on the centre of your chest. If you wish, you can supportively rub this area for soothing self-support. Notice how this makes you feel.

2. Enhance the soothing effect by inviting your body to release tension, freeing up your breathing and softening around the support of your hand. Allow your feelings to be there, reassuring yourself that you are safe now. It can help to remember that all emotions will pass eventually. They arrive, perhaps intensify then subside. If we observe the natural waves that emotions travel on, rather than trying to fight or resist them, they can feel more manageable. In this way,

we can grow our tolerance for emotional ups and downs, and our ability to hold ourselves through difficult feelings.

3. Choose to keep your hand on your chest or release it to a comfortable position in your lap or at your side for the rest of the exercise.

4. Stay with the feeling of soothing and softening for as long as feels good, or for as short as the time you have. Even a brief moment of self-support can change the course of an emotional reaction and help us return to our day with more kindness and clarity of mind.

Enquire

This is an invitation to ask ourselves what we need, or what our feelings or our situation needs, then be open to our mind's response.

1. Ask: 'What do I need right now?' or 'What does my situation need?'

2. Be open to the spontaneous response of your mind and feelings.

3. Aim to describe what feels needed, perhaps a quality you would love to have more of or would feel helpful. It could be strength, patience, kindness or whatever feels true.

  + If you find yourself answering in practical terms, like needing a cup of tea, go on to ask what the tea would bring you. Perhaps it's comfort and nurturing. Then work with the words 'comfort' and 'nurturing' for the rest of the exercise. This enquiry can feel satisfying in itself as a way to acknowledge your feelings and show caring towards your experience.

  + If you find yourself answering in negative terms, such as 'I need to feel less overwhelmed' or 'I need to be less nervous' then consider how you could express this positively. If you don't want to feel nervous, how do you want to feel? Maybe confident, peaceful or brave. Or if you want to feel less overwhelmed, what do you want to feel more of? Maybe more in control and trusting in yourself. It is important that your words feel true for you.

Wish well

1. This is an opportunity to turn your enquiry into a well-wish for yourself and others. If you felt a need for peace and relief from hurting, for example, you might say in your mind or out loud, 'May I find peace and relief.'

2. Then expand your awareness to include others. Take a moment to consider anyone else who might need peace and relief from hurting, and who might benefit from your well-wishes. Extend your wishes to them too. 'May … find peace and relief.' This will remind you that you are not alone in your pain – others also might hurt at this time like you do.

3. Extend your awareness further outwards to the level of shared humanity for an added boost to heartfelt strength. Perhaps extend your wishes outwards to all who might be experiencing pain or difficulty at this time, such as in your community, country or the world as a whole, or even simply express a wish to all living beings: 'May all who need it find peace and relief.' Find your own words that feel right for you and that might feel like energetic activism.

4. To close, fold the warmth and caring you have generated from your own heart back into yourself so you are filled. Take a deep breath and spend a few moments basking in these feelings before moving into your day or night.

A healing factor – compassion in action

According to research by Richard Davidson, true compassion practice is not just about holding an attitude of loving-kindness towards ourselves and others. It is also a disposition to want to do something to alleviate suffering. This is seen in the brains of meditation experts when they focus on compassion – areas of the brain light up that are involved in action.

The 'SEW' exercise encourages proactive compassion and is reinforced when we go out into the world and take actions that support it. This could be as small as placing a soothing hand on your own chest for some emotional soothing when you need it, or calling someone you care about to check in with them, or donating to your favourite charity. Or it could be carrying out random acts of kindness or pausing to send an energetic well-wish to those affected by events that might not affect you directly but touch your heart. It all adds towards building a habit of compassion towards yourself and others.

This shift in focus to how we can help ourselves and others runs counter to the tendency with depression to feel helpless and hopeless. Slowly but surely, it can uplift our spirits and build our confidence to overcome our challenges. It is good for our general health, too, with the stimulation of the wholesome ventral vagal pathway of our relaxation response.

Exercise 10.3

Quiet your mind, soothe your emotions and feel more present with self-supportive touch

Here are some self-supportive touch options for you to explore. Apply any of the positions for at least 30 seconds to give your brain enough time to soak up the experience. After experimenting with the different options and finding your favourites, you are welcome to stick with those. Try using a few or all of the holding positions in sequence (approximately 30 seconds each or more if you like) to enhance the soothing, relaxing effect, such as before sleep or at a break in your work day. Specifically when supporting depression, touch can not only be comforting, but it can also give us a subtle energy boost, waking us up to our sense of aliveness that can motivate us to invest in our well-being.

To quiet a busy mind

- Hold your hands on the sides of your head with the fingers touching the top of your head.
- Hold the back and front of your head.
- Give your neck and shoulders a brief rub or massage.

For some emotional soothing and comfort

- Place both hands over the centre of your chest or cross your arms over your chest, whichever feels best.
- Slip your hands under your armpits to hold the sides of your ribcage for this version of a self-hug.
- Rub your arms wherever it feels good.
- Give your lower back a rub with both hands; according to Chinese medicine, this can relieve fear.

To feel more present and grounded

- Rub your thighs.
- Hold your knees or rub circles around them for a few moments.
- Rub the bottoms of your feet on the ground with bare feet, or with your hands if you can easily reach your feet.

When you wish to be inconspicuous

- Hold your own hand, arm or even just a finger as firmly as you wish to help you feel calmer and more in control.
- Touch a hand to the centre of your chest for a few soothing moments.
- If you are sitting, place your hands on your thighs or above your knees, and give them a gentle or firmer squeeze (according to your preference) for some grounding.

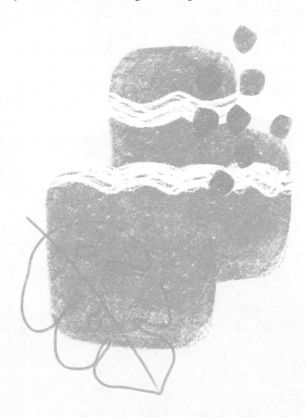

chapter 11

Depression toolkit:
Going deeper

'You can't go back and change the
beginning, but you can start where you
are and change the ending.' — **C.S. Lewis**

This chapter's stress toolkit:

Exercise 11.1   A visualisation for working with inner power struggles
and low self-worth

Exercise 11.2   List your triggers – reflecting on inner power
struggles from past and present

Exercise 11.3   Feeling physically stronger regarding difficult feelings

Exercise 11.4   Connecting with meaning and purpose

Exercise 11.5   Reflecting on a sense of belonging and ideas to
encourage it

 ometimes, there are deeper aspects of depression that need tending for upliftment to be sustainable. This chapter is designed to tend to those aspects, such as internal power struggles waging inside us that cause feelings such as shame or worthlessness. It includes several ways to explore this dynamic so as to step into greater confidence and self-worth. There is also an opportunity to connect with meaning and purpose for inspiration, motivation and encouragement to be proactive.

To reap maximum rewards from the practices in this chapter, it is optimal to allow 20–30 minutes to explore an exercise initially, then repeat those you like over time, perhaps more quickly for consolidation. Keeping a journal can be helpful to take notes along the way and provide a way to reflect back on progress over time. This is your record of the practices that worked well for you, which you can draw on in future to prevent relapse or whenever you want to bolster your learning and growth.

Depression as inner power struggle and ideas for reclaiming inner strength

An inner power struggle is a way of looking at and working with inner conflict. This could be something going on in our lives in the moment (such as when we negatively compare ourselves with others, or feel intimidated or ashamed). It could also be what is going on in our minds (such as when our own self-talk or inner critic belittles us and gives us a hard time). Emotions such as shame, sadness or anxiety can also trigger inner conflict or an inner power struggle when we might be afraid of, resist or feel overwhelmed by them. This can feel like fighting against our feelings, which can be exhausting and lead to feeling helpless or resigned about our ability to do anything about them. Sometimes our inner power struggles can run on autopilot, resulting in painful or difficult feelings such as confusion, shame, fear, anxiety or helplessness, which we might carry with us without being clear of the trigger.

Depression can reflect our inner power struggles. It can be a sign of making ourselves smaller or giving our power away, while making someone or something else bigger and more powerful in comparison. This could relate to feeling overpowered by someone or something bigger and stronger than us. Or it can relate to our thoughts, assumptions, feelings and memories. When we feel depressed, we are in a one-down or submissive position regarding something (such as a person, feeling or situation) that is in a one-up or dominant position in our minds or actual experience. With depression, we can fall into a habit of deflating our self-worth and feeling helpless or lesser at the slightest trigger, and believing nothing we do makes a difference. This inner power dynamic is what we are seeking to address in resolving patterns that may keep depression in place.

The exercises that follow include:

- **Exercise 11.1** A visualisation for working with inner power struggles and low self-worth
- **Exercise 11.2** List your triggers – reflecting on inner power struggles from past and present
- **Exercise 11.3** Feeling physically stronger regarding difficult feelings

The intention is to give you proactive strategies to turn your internal power struggles into opportunities for healing and growth. It is also so you can recognise more quickly when a power struggle may be affecting you, and feel more skilled at standing in your confidence and worth.

It is recommended to spend about 30 minutes or more the first time you try out these exercises, either one at a time or in combination. This could include time to write about your experience in a journal. Then you are welcome to return to any of the exercises as many times as you need until they feel complete. Your progress can grow and evolve over time, ultimately unravelling a tendency to shrink inside yourself or make yourself feel small in relation to difficult people, emotions or situations. The exercises are also an invitation to consider the kind of qualities you would like to embody when you do grow stronger.

Exercise 11.1

A visualisation for working with inner power struggles and low self-worth

Drawing on visualising your inner power dynamics, you are invited to explore how you might keep yourself small in your life, which might hold you back or keep depression in place.

1. Choose what to focus on.

You might start with a feeling that gets you down, such as worthlessness, helplessness, shame or envy, then recall one situation that led to your feeling this way. Or you can call to mind a person who you find intimidating and notice how you feel in their presence.

It is not advisable to choose your most triggering or traumatic memory to start with, because this might be overwhelming. Rather, choose a small- to medium-sized trigger so you can learn and grow from the experience. Perhaps you can start with an experience from childhood, such as a school peer who picked on you or a teacher you were scared of.

2. Play with sizes in your imagination.

Feel how small you might make yourself.

Call the triggering person or situation to mind. Notice how you feel, or used to feel in their presence. Then, in your imagination, consider if you could shrink to the size of your feelings while growing the other person or situation to the size of their dominance. How small would you be in relation to them?

With feelings like shame, guilt and fear, we might feel really small or invisible, with the intimidating person looming larger than life. Or we might place others on a pedestal and place ourselves on a lower level, as can happen with jealousy. Usually, when depression sets in so does this dynamic of tending to make ourselves feel small or ineffective, while possibly inflating the image of others or our life challenges.

Consider what kinds of behaviours, feelings and beliefs about yourself and life tend to emanate from feeling this way. What can you accomplish from this smallness and what can you not accomplish? Once you have a clear enough sense of this for now, pause to shake off the smallness. Take a deep breath to ready yourself for the next stage.

Grow yourself bigger in your imagination.

Now play in your imagination with growing yourself bigger in relation to the person or situation and seeing them shrinking. You might also wish to limit their influence by imagining placing them in a cage or box. How does this change how you feel and see the situation? What kind of authority does the person or situation have over you now? Does your confidence feel boosted? How might things have been different if you could have felt more confident in relation to the triggering person or situation?

Sometimes imagining growing in size can help us to see a bigger picture or new perspective that was not evident when we were small. How do you see yourself and your situation now? Stay with this image for a few moments and consider what kinds of behaviours, thoughts and beliefs could emanate from there.

From this bigger perspective, what could you accomplish that you might not have been able to when you felt smaller? You could say a statement about this in your mind or actually speak out loud to the other person or situation as a whole, such as saying 'No!' or 'You can't hurt me anymore.' Notice how even just imagining doing so can shift how you feel about yourself and the situation. You could also become curious about the other person's motivation for acting how they do, perhaps from their insecurities or need for power at someone else's expense.

3. Choose your size.

As a final step, feel the size that you ideally would like to be in relation to the previously triggering person or situation. You might not want to remain in a position of looming large over them or feeling bigger than you are comfortable with. Or perhaps staying with bigness for a while is something you are curious about to build your confidence. What size feels just right for you?

Maybe you wish to stand eye-to-eye and notice how you feel in the person's presence, holding your ground without shrinking. Maybe this process can give you back a piece of yourself or your worth that you did not even know was missing until now.

4. To close – at least for now.

Take a deep breath and stretch out your body before moving on with your day. You are also welcome to make a few notes in your journal about what you experienced. If you wish to continue to reflect on inner power dynamics that you may carry regarding past and present triggers, you can move on to Exercise 11.2.

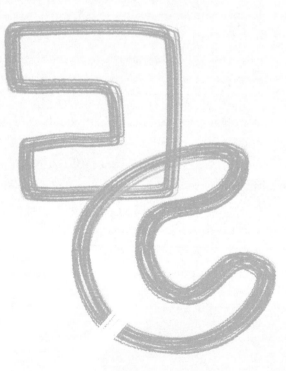

Memory reconsolidation

The technical term for revisiting our long-term memories in a way that produces transformational change is memory reconsolidation. It requires being in touch with our feelings while revisiting our memories, and proactively imagining or enacting new outcomes that shift how we feel in relation to what happened. While this does not change what happened, it can change how we respond emotionally and in our behaviour. The process opens a window of opportunity where the brain is malleable. It allows for new neural pathways to form and mesh with the old ones that are associated with the particular memory. As a result, when we reactivate the memory in future, the new and more empowering outcomes are tied in.

How we translate this into action in our lives is then up to us, bearing in mind that the main gift is to our personal growth, so we might not actually need to confront people from our past, unless it feels important.

When we work with our triggers, we might meet a need to forgive ourselves, or be willing to accept aspects of ourselves as we explore stepping into greater self-worth. This journey might not be easy, and growth might be incremental. But gradual and mindful growth can be more sustainable than a one-off breakthrough.

Exercise 11.2

List your triggers – reflecting on inner power struggles from past and present

This is an opportunity to reflect on the kinds of dynamics that tend to trigger your feeling insecure or small. It can let you become more skilled at spotting triggers in future and with the help of this chapter's exercises also become more skilled at staying grounded and centred when faced with similar situations.

Having a pen and paper or a journal handy for writing your reflections can be a helpful way to record what you discover. This can serve for future reference and can be added to whenever you catch yourself triggered in a new way. Then choose one or two of these themes to run through exercises 11.1 and 11.3, aiming to take power back and build inner strength and confidence.

1. Different kinds of triggers.

- Most of us have experienced challenging relationship dynamics at some point in our lives when we might have felt intimidated, overpowered or made to feel lesser than. We might have social triggers such as criticism, rejection or feeling left out, and this is possible even when others are not aware of how we feel around them.

- Our triggers can involve negative comparisons. This might apply on a physical level, such as body shape, height, physical ability, the appearance of fitness or a view of what is attractive. Or it might apply to comparing ourselves in relation to an aspect of life, such as the appearance of success, level of education, intellect, accomplishment, age, artistic ability or a personality characteristic like asscrtiveness. This can apply even when others are not aware of how we feel around them.

- We can also fall prey to inanimate triggers, such as money or a feeling of overwhelm in relation to life in general, which can happen with depression.

- What might your triggers be?

2. Reflection idea – create a timeline of triggers from childhood to adulthood.

- When you were very young, did you have a domineering sibling or a family dynamic that rendered you feeling less than? Or maybe there was a medical issue that felt overwhelming, such as being in hospital, or a physical challenge was the antagonist.

- In later childhood, were there conflict situations that you may have encountered at home or school, such as an intimidating teacher or bullying?

- In your adult years, have you experienced triggering work situations, like an opportunity lost to someone else, or a manager or colleague who gave you a hard time? In your personal life, did a relationship end badly and leave you feeling less than? Or was there an incident or event that felt overwhelming? Or has money been triggering for you and since when?

Choose one of these dynamics at a time to work with in exercises 11.1 and 11.3. In this way, you can explore righting the power dynamic in your mind and memory to the extent that feels possible at this time and towards feeling stronger in yourself. This can help you to claim back pieces of yourself that stack one on top of the other to grow your confidence and self-worth.

A few notes: Remember not to tackle anything that feels too traumatic on your own. If this is the case, seek professional support for those memories and use the exercises in this chapter to work with triggers that feel more manageable.

Over time, you can work with different memories until your belief in your value and ability to stand up for yourself feels sufficiently bolstered. As you go along, each memory can transform into an empowering one that can build one on top of the other to grow your self-esteem and confidence. Each time you run through these exercises, they might go more quickly as you become familiar with stepping into your power. As your self-confidence grows, you might also find that you do not need to work with every memory and can generalise to different challenging situations.

3. Working with inanimate triggers

Working with an inanimate object such as money is the same as working with any trigger. If money intimidates you, for example, you could visualise money in front of you, perhaps looming large or however feels true. Then imagine speaking with it and considering what it might take to right the power dynamic or befriend it so you can have a healthier relationship with money, making and managing it more confidently. This might also include reflecting on beliefs you might have inherited from those you grew up with.

4. You may not be able to take power back from some situations.

It is possible to realise that we cannot deal with some power dynamics on our own or necessarily take our power back from them. These might be situations far bigger than us individually. Acknowledging this can motivate us to seek the help we need or join supportive communities to help rebuild our sense of worth, perhaps together with fresh determination and support to do what is possible, let go of what we can emotionally, and move on with our lives more confidently.

Exercise 11.3

Feeling physically stronger in relation to difficult feelings

This exercise builds on the previous ones. With it, you can embody your path to feeling more empowered regarding your triggers. It can facilitate growing a physical sense of strength and ability to make a difference regarding inner power dynamics. Like the previous exercises, this exercise works best when you allocate uninterrupted time for it. Perhaps allow 15–30 minutes for an initial exploration that you can follow up with at a later time, which can include time to write about your experience afterwards in a journal if you wish.

1. Choose what to focus on.

You could continue to focus on a dynamic identified in Exercise 11.1 or 11.2, or identify one triggering situation that comes to mind now. A reminder not to work with the most triggering or traumatic circumstances on your own because this can be re-traumatising. Professional support is recommended for addressing traumatic experience. What this exercise can facilitate is a gradual building of inner strength that can support you in facing bigger triggers and buffer you against future triggers.

2. Mark the start of your exploration.

Take a deep breath. This can help you shift gears from your usual awareness to focusing more intently on what you are about to explore.

3. Embody or enact the process of moving from small to big and somewhere in between.

Being small

When you hold in mind a memory of feeling triggered or disempowered in some way, notice the feelings that churn up inside you. Perhaps feelings like shame, guilt, defeat or resignation show up. Then notice how your body might want to shape around these feelings. Does your spine want to hunch over and your chest and shoulders close inwards? Do you lower your head or try to hide like a tortoise in its shell, or do you leave your body, trying to be invisible or disappearing from what is going on?

Allow your body to shrink to the size of your feelings or take shape around your feelings. Notice where in your body you feel the experience most, such as in your throat, the middle of your belly, a part of your back or in the furrow between your brows. There is no right or wrong, just what you truly feel. You might also notice how emotions or any feelings might appear or disappear, perhaps sadness, anger, confusion or feeling nothing at all. Or perhaps you find your mind slipping off to a peaceful place. You might consider, 'Who do I become when I feel small in this way?' or 'What am I capable or not capable of when I feel this way?' Let your mind respond as it will.

Feeling into being big

Here, you are invited to shake off smallness and play with stepping into a different role, that of the bigger, dominant person as if stepping into their shoes and imagining becoming them. This could be experienced humorously or feel scary as you try to find it in yourself to 'become them' in this embodied experimental way.

You might consider, if the power play were captured in a photograph, what posture would they be holding? Would their arms and hands be open or crossed? Would their finger be pointing at you? What is their facial expression? You might exaggerate their posture and facial expression to help you get a better feel for them, like you were an actor in a play. How is it for you to experiment in this way? Could you enter into the position easily or was it difficult? What might you be able to see or understand from this dominant or bigger perspective?

Then when you are ready, take a moment to shake off this playing with bigness so as to explore the next step of moving between being big and small in an authentic, organic way.

Move between big and small

Start in the position of being small. Then move between the polarities of being small and big. But this time, allow your body to gradually and organically discover its strength to grow out of or break free from feeling small. Move in a slow and mindful way. Moving more slowly is recommended so you can stay in touch with your body, meet any resistance to growing bigger and find the parts of your body receptive to growth. For example, this might be starting in a posture of defeat and gradually finding your way to a posture of greater courage and confidence. The outcome, once we are able to make this transition in a way that feels authentic, can be sustainable inner strength and resilience in relation to the trigger. It can also grow trust in our ability in general to rise up when we feel down.

Repeat three times or more if you like to get to physically know the transition between these contrasting positions.

Movements will evolve in their own way. For some this might involve a linear process of rising up in posture; for others it might be more circular, growing bigger and shrinking smaller a number of times until the transition feels more comfortable in relation to the triggering memory.

Consider a middle ground between the two extremes of big and small. A middle ground can represent being the kind of person we admire and respect, rather than perhaps inflating ourselves beyond what we feel comfortable with, or taking the place of the 'one-upper'. A quote from Brené Brown expresses this well: 'Don't shrink, don't puff, stand your sacred ground.' To find a middle ground that feels just right for now, transition a few more times between big and small to let your body feel into your favourite place in between – standing your sacred ground in a way that feels authentic.

Tips for finding strength and freedom from the inside out:

- ○ **Alternate between effort and relaxation** As you allow your body to grow from being small, explore pushing down into the ground through your feet and unfolding your spine until you reach a bigger position. Then reverse the process, so you can become familiar with how your body shrinks again. This can be how you proceed for a few repetitions. You can use your arms too, such as pressing downwards or gesturing 'No' to feel into setting a strong boundary, and alternating effort and relaxation to reinforce your sense of strength.

○ **Push** The physical experience of pushing against something can be helpful to feeling stronger in relation to our memories and emotions. To encourage this, explore pushing against the floor with your feet, against a wall with your arms or even pushing down into your seat in a way that feels strengthening regarding your memories and emotions. This is something you can return to play with any time you wish for a quick boost to inner strength. Even while sitting at your desk or cooking in the kitchen, it is a way to consolidate your progress out of the context of the full Exercise 11.3.

○ **Twist, spiral, wriggle** It is also possible to encounter a need to wriggle, twist or spiral our way out of or into positions. The aim is then to disentangle our body's sense of restriction and seek a greater sense of freedom. For example, as a brave literal interpretation of this exercise, Holocaust survivor Edith Eger shares in her book, *The Gift*, how at one point in her therapy process, she asked her therapist to hold her down. The intention was to allow her the physical experience of fighting and wriggling her way to a stronger sense of freedom.

○ **Body cues for future reference** As you go along, it can be helpful to pay attention to physical cues that you can use to unwind from stress: For example, you might take particular note of how your body feels different when you stand into more of your worth or courage. Perhaps your feet feel more grounded and your spine feels stronger, maybe you can breathe more freely – whatever feels true. You can draw on these physical cues to unwind on-the-spot into more confidence any time you need it.

○ **If anxiety rises up** As you explore growing bigger, it is possible that anxiety rises up with a fear of being bigger and more visible than you previously may have been comfortable with. This can be a natural part of the process of rising out of depression. The anxiety toolkit in chapters 4–6 can be helpful to support your progress, as can the short body-based practices in Chapter 10, such as SEW-ing yourself back together with some self-compassion when you need it.

4. Mark the close of your exploration for now.

Take a slow, deep breath into your new posture, allowing your breath to nourish you from head to toe. You might also ask yourself how you would like to use your new empowerment well today and in line with your values. Is there something you wish to do and what might that be? Then move on with your day, carrying your new embodied awareness with you.

Repeat the exercise as many times as you wish over a period of time as you continue to build your strength, break free from that which is holding you back and practise rising up from positions of smallness as you might encounter them.

Drawing on your body to unwind from a stress response

About the physical aspect of feeling stronger regarding our memories, this process draws on our body's innate ability to know what it needs to do towards freeing up blocked energy. This might be noticing what our bodies wanted to do but could not in the moment, as well as following our body's organic process of unwinding from a stress response.

Somatic psychologist and trauma expert Dr Arielle Schwartz explains that 'the body does not just hold the memory of what happened to us, it holds the memory of what wanted to happen.' For example, if a person is threatened and wanted to kick, scream or run away, but was not able to for fear of making a bad situation worse, they may have surrendered into helplessness. This might have been the best and safest option at the time. Later, when the time is right, we can revisit our memories with the intention of tuning into what our body wanted to do in relation to the overpowering force and before the moment of giving up. Usually, it involves a slow and mindful process, and for traumatic memories, it is advisable to work with a skilled professional.

Exercise 11.4

Connecting with meaning and purpose

What gives your life meaning and purpose? Or what could make life feel worthwhile? As humans, we tend to seek out meaning and purpose naturally; sometimes we lose touch with our ability to do so. This can be both a cause and a symptom of depression. When we rediscover our ability to feel purposeful and act in meaningful ways, it can be just the medicine we need to protect against depression. Getting started and realising what kinds of actions help us feel inspired, relevant and contributory can be the hardest part; sometimes soul searching is needed. Then the experiences themselves can motivate us to continue. Meaning and purpose can also evolve over time and look different at different stages of life.

Connecting with something – anything – we want to live for can compel us to want to survive even extremely stressful circumstances. This could be living for a loved one, for a particular contribution we wish to make to others or our world, or for goals or dreams we wish to achieve. It can ignite a flame of determination in our hearts and fuel a fighting spirit. It can give all of us a good reason to get out of bed in the morning and go about our day.

Some of us carry lofty ideas about meaning and purpose, perhaps believing that they need to be linked to a clear gift or talent that we may or may not have. The truth is that the simplest things that come most naturally to us can feed our sense of meaning and purpose.

Meaning and purpose from making any contribution

Even if we do not track down our interests and talents for deeper meaning and purpose, we can create meaning and purpose in other ways. This could be through actions that warm our hearts, make us feel good about what we have done and help us go to sleep feeling good about our day. It could be taking care of children, keeping up a clean home or doing some DIY.

It could be making a call to a family member when they need it, or a friend we have not spoken to in a while, or supporting a charity that touches our hearts. It could be volunteering our time in ways that feel meaningful, such as at an animal shelter, on a school committee or in our community. It could be helping a frail person across the road or adding more self-care into our routine.

These kinds of actions are not always considered as sources of meaning and purpose, but they can feel deeply purposeful and uplifting in the moment. They are not necessarily linked to our talents, but do link to an attitude of caring that can give us a great sense of purpose, pleasure and satisfaction.

It is also possible that we long to connect with our particular gifts or talents, or just feel that something is missing in our lives. Could it be that you have lost touch with something you enjoyed long ago? Or is there room you can make for a hobby that can bring you joy and meaning? In your heart you know the answers, even if you need to do some soul searching or reflecting back on something you may have lost touch with, or possibly something new that really interests you and that you wish to incorporate in your life in some way.

Here is a visualisation journey that can stimulate this kind of thinking about your particular talents:

1. Imagine you and a group of people are stranded on an island.

Imagine arriving there on a boat and finding your way over the first days, weeks and months to establishing the basics of your lives on the island. All hands will be needed initially to help with mapping out the landscape, building shelters to sleep in, and sourcing and preparing food to eat. That should give everyone enough of a sense of meaning and purpose to start with in support of the greater good.

2. Notice natural talents and interests.

Once the initial orientation period wears off and you begin to settle down, ask yourself, 'What am I drawn to do to make a contribution?' 'If I could do anything at all, what would it be?' You might notice whether you are naturally drawn to a particular role or activity on the island. Are you the chef, the farmer, the builder, or the architect? Are you the decorator with an eye for creating beauty? Are you the entertainer, or the one who brings people together to talk about issues or plans? Are you a spiritual guide, teacher of certain skills, child minder, animal whisperer, doctor or nurse?

You might imagine scenarios unfolding like a movie in your mind. It could be like starting over, regardless of what you might have busied yourself with in the past. Maybe you are drawn to a few different tasks, which is fine if you have the energy and time to do them all.

3. Come back to your current life off the island.

Ask yourself if you would change anything or leave it the same. Are you aware of anything you could include now in your life to re-route towards a greater sense of meaning and purpose? Can you utilise your talents more fully or follow your interests more? When we are young, we might have discovered particular talents and abilities, and later in life we can discover new aspects of ourselves. What have these interests been?

If we stray too far from our natural talents and interests, perhaps landing in a life expected of us by others or a life just for money, then of course we can lose touch with a sense of deeper meaning and purpose. Fortunately, this is something we can reconnect with at any time with some soul searching and reflecting on our interests. Then we can chart a way forwards that makes space for this in any form that works for us, such as a hobby, a shared interest group, volunteering in some meaningful way, or even changing our vocation.

It is not what we do or the size of our actions that matter most. It is about anything, big or small, that can regularly remind us that we have something to offer, that we can make a difference in our own lives and the lives of others and that life is very much worth living.

Exercise 11.5

Reflecting on a sense of belonging and ideas to encourage it

Who am I and where do I fit in? These are fundamental human questions that can lead us in all sorts of directions in search of answers. With a sense of belonging, we can feel good about ourselves, likeable and contributory, which can go on to feed a sense of meaning and purpose. Without it, we can feel all alone in life – like we are not okay, unlikeable, not good enough or have nothing to offer. This can be a slippery slope into depression. Or it can drive the polar opposite of depression, which can be fervent activism to take a strong and vocal stand for what we believe in when this goes against the status quo.

Our human species organises itself around this sense of belonging, built on the experience of feeling valued and welcomed, fitting in, and sharing values and views on life. This could relate to family, religion, spirituality, hobbies, cities, nationalities and political parties. Those with like minds tend to validate and support each other, although sometimes this is to the exclusion and rejection of others.

We cannot separate a sense of belonging from our physical and mental health. A sense of belonging can bolster a sense of safety and feeling good about ourselves and our lives. It can help us manage daily stresses and reassure us about the choices we make. People are more resilient to bounce back from difficult times when they have other people they can turn to and feel understood by.

Attachment and belonging

A sense of belonging can have roots in our early years and the quality of attachment, attentiveness and care we experienced from our caregivers. Studies have shown a link, for example, between emotional neglect or significant mis-attunement in our formative years, with qualities such as low self-esteem, a negative view of life, and a tendency to be mistrustful and assume rejection quickly when it might not be real. Later life experiences can go on to heal or injure our self-esteem as we accumulate healing or hurtful experiences. These either validate or invalidate our sense of self and worth.

Our identity and temperament can also be different from those we are surrounded by to distinguish us and have us feel a need to validate who and how we are. It is also true that certain kinds of people tend to be welcomed in the social status quo while others are marginalised or treated unfairly. This can make life all the more difficult in the effort for authentic self-expression.

There are many who walk through life feeling different, like they don't fit in. Here are a few ideas to boost a sense of belonging to help counteract the kind of depression deeply influenced by feeling that we do not belong:

1. Never give up on believing there are like-minded people to be found.

With this in mind, keep mustering up the energy to make an effort. Even if it feels uncomfortable at first, this might be the very thing needed to discover who we resonate with. As much as we are all individuals, there are always like-minded people somewhere to be found. This effort might also be well directed when we may need it, towards finding support in the form of someone we can talk to about our challenges, which could be a friend, a mental health professional or someone in our community, rather than bottling up our feelings.

2. Get up, dust yourself off and try again.

We all get discouraged along the way by interactions with others. Just because we have a horrible experience one day, tomorrow might be different – we might connect with people who would love to have us as part of their group.

3. Keep an open mind.

Try new activities, seek out groups with common interests and allow yourself to strike up a conversation with the different people you meet.

4. Accept who you are.

This can be a difficult task. Remember that we are all different and nobody is perfect. Trying to be someone we're not won't win us a sense of belonging in a lasting way. A soothing practice, which you can try out if you are feeling down and struggling with self-acceptance, is the compassion practice in Chapter 10, to 'SEW' yourself back together again. You might make a point of looking for similarities rather than focusing on differences between people around you as possible points of connection.

Many universal human qualities can be helpful here. For example, we all experience stress and when stressed we can fall prey to a scarcity mentality, which might be what lies underneath the human experience of 'us and them' and fear of 'the other'. This is as opposed to ideals such as warm-hearted acceptance of each other, celebration of difference and collaboration towards mutual win–win solutions. We are hardwired to light up inside with a smile that we might give (even to ourselves) and receive (even from a stranger).

The 'SEW' practice in Chapter 10 can be a wonderful practice. Try using it once a day for a while to inspire your smiles. Doing so can help soothe your troubles, remind you to hold your head up high and lead from your heart, and encourage you to keep going.

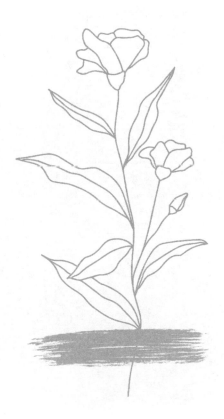

Part 3

Shared toolkit for anxiety and depression

chapter 12

Visualisations for inner guidance and inspiration

'The best use of imagination is creativity. The worst use of imagination is anxiety.' — **Deepak Chopra**

This chapter's stress toolkit:

Here is a menu for applying visualisation for different purposes. Choose from these options and go to those you feel drawn to. Return to other options at another time.

Soothing, protection and inspiration (six short options)

Exercise 12.1 Colour

Exercise 12.2 Protective bubble

Exercise 12.3 Held between earth and sky

Exercise 12.4 A safe place

Exercise 12.5 Eye-to-eye inspiration

Exercise 12.6 Tuning into the air around you for upliftment and inspiration

Your best future self (two options)

Exercise 12.7 Meeting a positive vision of yourself later in life in two stages

Exercise 12.8 Tuning into inspiring goals for 10 years in the future and working back to present time

Healing and inward reflection (two options)

Exercise 12.9 A healing visualisation – take the hand of your younger self and walk it into present time

Exercise 12.10 Surprise me! A brief inner journey

hen we are depressed or anxious, we have limited access to the creative scope of our imagination, which we need for flexible, open-minded thinking. Rigid, fixed thinking patterns can set in with limiting, negative beliefs about ourselves, others and life. Visualisation is a practice that can loosen up these rigid patterns, opening our minds to new possibilities and sparking hope. It can also offer relief or resolution from challenges that we might face, because it invites us to see things differently. As Albert Einstein said, 'We can't solve problems by using the same kind of thinking we used when we created them.'

We live in a world full of distractions with constant news, entertainment and social media to add to those generated in our own minds. It is hard to remain focused on what matters most or feel connected with ourselves in a deeper way. This is another gift that visualisation practices can offer, helping us connect in with ourselves in meaningful ways.

Visualisation is the mental process of imagining different scenarios and outcomes. It has been used since ancient times; for example, many cultures have practices that incorporate visualisation processes for mystical and healing purposes. Nowadays, CEOs, athletes and seekers of personal growth use it, and there is extensive research to back its effectiveness as a tool to support healing, personal growth and achieving our goals.

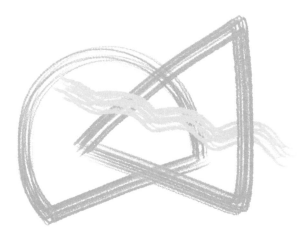

How does visualisation work?

Visualisation works by shifting awareness out of rational, logical, linear thinking and into the wide-open field of dream-like possibility. On its own, this can have a stress-relieving effect that, according to dream expert Dr Gerald Epstein, is required for emotional healing. Our images can also be transferred back into life as new ways of thinking to inform our sense of self and the choices we make. If you were to play for a moment with the power of your imagination to influence how you feel, you can compare the following scenarios. Imagine a worst-case scenario in an area of your life and let it unfold in your mind. You might notice visceral fear building up inside you. Now imagine the best possible outcome in an area of your life and notice how your feelings shift, perhaps from fear towards happiness. Quite simply, life can feel better when we align with uplifting, inspiring mental imagery.

Often the hardest step in change is the first one. Visualisation can facilitate this first step. 'If you can visualize yourself happy and healthy, then you already possess the strength to move beyond the struggle.' Tessa Koller, writer and motivational speaker, shared this regarding her struggle with depression and the key role visualisation played in her process of overcoming it. We are the only ones who can do this for ourselves, nobody else's imagination or creativity can do it for us.

Setting up for a visualisation practice
General recommendations for all visualisations

1. Relax

Our imagination functions best when we feel relaxed and when we can carve out time to be uninterrupted. This could be a couple of precious minutes in our day or longer for those visualisations that take us on a journey.

2. Find a comfortable position

You can lie down or sit in a comfortable chair.

3. Timing

This is up to you and the time you have. Some practices take longer, or when completed once, they can be recalled in a shorter amount of time. Other practices are shorter and can take just a minute or two.

4. When your mind wanders or you struggle to concentrate

With kindness, return your attention to the task at hand, no matter how many times this might happen. As humans our minds will wander!

5. Eyes closed or softly open

To focus inwards on the visualisation and avoid distraction, keep your eyes closed or softly focused in front of you. For the sake of reading the instructions, you can read and visualise in alternation.

6. One to three deep breaths to start

Once you are comfortable and ready to start, you are invited to open any of the practices with one to three slow breaths. This marks the transition from where your mind is to focus on the journey that it is about to embark on.

7. One to three breaths to close

To mark the conclusion of the experience, it can be helpful to take one to three slow, deep breaths, marking the transition between visualisation and your usual consciousness.

8. Journaling after a visualisation

This is optional. Writing down thoughts, reflections and insights can consolidate the experience. This especially applies to the visualisations for your best future self and healing, as well as to take note of any insights you might discover through the visualisations.

Soothing, protection and inspiration

Here are six short visualisation options to try out. Each can be expanded into a longer practice for as long as feels good. Or they can be made portable to call upon when you wish to do so.

Timing: 2–5 minutes per practice.

Exercise 12.1

Colour

What colour feels beneficial or soothing for you today? Any colour or combination of colours will do.

1. Imagine surrounding yourself with this colour/s, which might also have a texture that feels good, such as airy pinks or cloudy light blues. Or you might enjoy an image that conjures up a colour, such as being surrounded in sunshine or soaking in a warm aquamarine ocean, or taking in the earthy forest shades and smells, or perhaps supercharging your energy with some fiery reds and yellows. This could be whatever resonates with you at the time as a colour or a richly textured sensory experience.

2. Notice how you feel with this colour around you and perhaps extending as far outwards as feels right.

3. To enhance the experience, you could turn it into a breathing meditation to infuse yourself with this colour. To do so, slow down your breathing and with each inhalation draw the colour into your body. As you breathe out, imagine your breath spreading the colour outwards around you. Repeat three to nine times, noticing how this affects your mind and mood and might enhance your colour visualisation.

Exercise 12.2

Protective bubble

This visualisation can provide a sense of emotional containment while also helping you to clear your mind and feel more centred in yourself.

1. Imagine a protective bubble surrounding you, like it is delineating your personal space as near or far from you as feels right today. What colour would you like it to be? What texture and how thick, thin or porous do you wish your bubble to be?

2. Allow time for constructing the bubble around you three dimensionally – front and back, both sides, above and below so it feels intact. If it feels porous in places, this could reflect things on your mind that might be piercing into your personal space. If so, kindly ask those people or situations to step outside of your bubble and wait there until you are ready to focus on them. This can be carried out quickly or take a bit longer, depending on your nature and the intensity of what you are dealing with. Then you can fill in and strengthen the weak parts of the bubble to create more security and spaciousness in your personal space.

3. Pause when your bubble is intact to consider how you feel inside of it. Can you breathe more easily and do you feel you have more space to be yourself?

This visualisation can be helpful as a centring or calming practice before an important meeting or to prepare you for working with people (such as teaching, facilitation, coaching, therapy, etc.) or whenever you might need to clear your mind.

Physically delineating your bubble with your hands can help to boost a sense of inner strength in your ability to set this boundary around yourself. Try extending your arms outwards to delineate the boundary around you with your hands. Notice what this might add to your protective bubble experience.

Exercise 12.3

Held between earth and sky

For a quick boost to personal strength and feeling held in a larger, nature-based context, you can draw on the image of standing or sitting tall between earth and sky. You can also imagine your own North Star up in the sky somewhere directly above your head, which is always there for you to align with.

This visualisation is inspired by an ancient Eastern wisdom practice of working through the body's vertical alignment to connect with the wider perspective of nature and the greater universe. Start by grounding through your feet then feel uplifted through the crown of your head. Together, this gives your uprightness a two-way elongation – the ground's stability on one end and the sky's vast, expansiveness on the other.

How might this simple practice shift your frame of mind? Perhaps you notice your awareness slipping out of worries and into more open-mindedness as you see a bigger picture that you can apply back into your life. Adding the image of your own personal North Star can also boost a sense of higher purpose, reminding you of what matters most and perhaps also kindling some fresh inspiration.

Exercise 12.4

A safe place

We cannot always feel safe in ourselves or in our lives. Having an imaginary safe place to take refuge for calm and emotional soothing can remind our bodies and minds that feeling safe is possible while nourishing our wholesome relaxation response to bolster our sense of well-being. When we feel calmer, we can think more clearly, logically and intuitively about the situations we face. When you have imagined a safe space into which you can retreat in your mind, you can call upon it whenever you wish for the calm that it can provide.

To visualise a safe place that resonates with you, here are some tips to guide your thinking:

1. What is your favourite place where you tend to feel safe and perhaps able to let go of your worries? Are you surrounded by nature, or perhaps at home or with certain people? It could be a real or imaginary place – anywhere that feels truly comforting for you. Perhaps mentally scroll through the options if a few places come to mind, until you find the one that feels best.

2. Immerse yourself more fully in the experience by noticing details through all your senses, such as looking around, noticing sensations like the temperature of the air, listening to sounds, noticing smells or tastes, and even tuning into your intuitive sixth sense about how you feel while being there. Allow your body to relax into the experience. Notice where you would like to position yourself in your environment so you feel most comfortable.

3. You can enhance the experience by breathing in the air from this safe space and breathing out any negativity or worries. Breathe slowly to increase the relaxing effect. Then pause – how do you feel? And where in your body do you feel it most? You can tune into this for ease and relaxation any time you need it.

4. To close, you might offer a thank you to the experience before taking a deep breath to transition back into your day.

Exercise 12.5

Eye-to-eye inspiration

When we meet the eyes of those who love or inspire us, it can have a naturally uplifting, antidepressant effect. Sometimes we avoid eye contact when we feel down, but it can be the very thing to lift us out of a stupor. The more we can spontaneously allow for this – to catch and perhaps hold eye contact for a few moments longer than usual – the more we can top up on our upliftment. You can also try looking at a photograph showing the face and eyes of someone significant for a few moments of heart-warming support.

As a visualisation:

- Call someone to mind whose support or inspiration you feel you could benefit from at this time. It could be a family member, a special friend, or an inspiring teacher or leader. Imagine their eyes shining as they look towards you with acceptance and caring. How does it feel? There are times when, instead of acceptance and caring, you might need a boost of courage. You can also get this through the eyes of another. Perhaps it is a passionate, fiery activist you know, whose fierceness can embolden you. Whose eyes are just right to lift your spirits today?

- Breathe naturally or take a few deep breaths as you imagine an energy exchange between your eyes and those of another for a few mindful moments.

Exercise 12.6

Tuning into the air around you for upliftment and inspiration

- Imagine that the air around you is coming alive with the shimmering glow of sunshine golds and moonshine silvers (no matter what time it is). Open yourself to the warmth and perhaps a rush of awe and curiosity as if something wonderful is happening. You might even sense you are looking into a dimension beyond the ordinary. In many traditions, air is considered to carry vital energy or life force; this visualisation is a way to connect with this idea and possibly the energising feeling of vitality that it can provide.

- With each breath, imagine breathing this life-giving, glistening air into and out of yourself. Notice how far inside you it reaches with each in-breath, and how far it extends outwards with each out-breath. Invite your body to become filled gradually from head to toe with this shimmering vitality, and feel surrounded and protected by its warmth and radiance.

- If you wish, play with scooping this air with your hands to draw it into parts of your body that you feel need it – maybe your heart, belly, head, lower back or any part that needs some support.

- Pause to notice how you feel before moving on with your day.

Your best future self

This is an invitation to visualise your best life. Doing so can counteract a tendency to keep yourself small with negative comparisons.

Exercise 12.7 is an opportunity to meet a positive vision of yourself later in life in two stages, including much later for the perspective this can bring. It represents your life having turned out really well. As part of the exercise, you will be invited to ask for encouragement and guidance to work towards these outcomes from where you are now.

Exercise 12.8 is an opportunity to tune into inspiring goals, starting 10 years into the future and working back to present time. From this, you can identify supportive actions in line with your goals.

Exercise 12.7

Meeting a positive vision of yourself later in life in two stages

Timing: 10–20 minutes, including journaling time if you like

1. Imagine walking along a road.

Your first stop is a house along the way in which your future self lives, who is 10 years older than you are now. This is a future self for whom life has turned out really well. Stop by and imagine them coming out to greet you. What do you notice about them and perhaps the house they live in?

2. Ask them some questions.

You could ask how they spend their time and what they have achieved. How do they feel about their life? What piece of advice do they have about what you need to do to achieve this wonderful future self? You might reflect on some action steps that you could take towards it from present time.

3. Walk further down the road.

Keep walking until you come to a house in which your best future self lives, who is much older than you are now. Maybe you meet your 80-year-old self, or your 100-year-old self if you already are nearing 80. You can go through the same process of noticing who this person is and what kind of house they live in, and you could ask for advice from their mature perspective. Our priorities and outlooks change as we get older. So your future self 10 years down the line might have different advice for you than your 80- or 100-year-old self. Notice who they are and listen to the advice they offer you.

4. Write down your key takeaways from this visualisation.

This will help you remember the experience and reflect back on it later. To take your thinking even further, refer to the STEPS model in Chapter 15, to guide how to think through and plan the changes you wish to make in the shorter and longer term in line with the advice you just received.

Note: Carrying out an exercise like this can lead to conversations and reflections about what feels most important in life, and can spark meaningful changes. Or it might simply be affirming of the path you are on, which can boost your self-confidence.

Exercise 12.8

Tuning into inspiring goals for 10 years in the future and working back to present time

Timing: 15–30 minutes, including journaling time if you like

To add to the visualisation in Exercise 12.7, or to use separately, this is an invitation to tune into the best possible outcomes for yourself 10 years from now and work backwards to present time. This represents a potentially aspirational and inspirational future vision, which can motivate you towards achieving it. It also involves breaking down best outcomes into longer- and shorter-term goals and action steps.

1. Visualise your best future self and life 10 years from now. Take your time to picture this as clearly as you can, as it pertains to different aspects of yourself and your life, personally and professionally, materially and spiritually – add whatever details feel relevant.

2. Work backwards in stages, picturing in the same detail what you and your life look and feel like 5 years then 2 years from now, and all the way to present time.

3. Identify accessible choices you could make in line with your vision. The STEPS model in Chapter 15 can help you here.

Being inspired and motivated by your best possible self

This exercise is inspired by a well-researched practice introduced by Laura King in 2001. This practice of visualising and writing down what King refers to as your 'Best Possible Self' is seen to significantly improve your self-esteem, sense of well-being and agency as the creator of your life. For good results, King suggests writing for 20 minutes a day and repeating the process for 4 days in a row. Psychology professor Timothy Wilson recommends going into detail about what you ideally see yourself achieving, as well as the steps you took to get there at each stage of your future projection. This includes reference to the work it takes to achieve your goals.

Healing and inward reflection

In the first of these last two visualisation practices, you will turn from meeting your future self to healing your past self and bringing that healing into the present. The second allows you to be guided by whatever direction your mind chooses to take – it's a chance for spontaneous self-reflection.

Exercise 12.9

A healing visualisation – take the hand of your younger self and walk it to present time

Timing: 10–15 minutes, or less once familiar with the exercise, plus journaling time afterwards if you like

The intention with this visualisation is to imagine meeting a younger version of yourself at a time and place when you felt vulnerable or needed support, and imagine bringing them back with you into present time.

When you are feeling down, you might try this out. Consider whether your current feelings might have roots somewhere in your past. If you pick up on a time you felt this way when you were younger, aim to track down your earliest memory of feeling this way, then try out this visualisation with curiosity about how this might support you even now. Or you could use this visualisation any time to bolster your sense of maturity and progress regarding any memory of your younger self needing some support.

1. Remind yourself of the adult you are now.

Sit or stand in the qualities that represent your maturity, self-awareness or self-confidence, which might be greater than when you were younger. You can remind yourself of your achievements and positive qualities to help you here. Then take a breath to transition into the following visualisation.

2. Reflect back on a stressful or vulnerable time for your younger self.

You might have been very young or it could be just a few years ago. You might recall one incident or a set of incidents. Choose one memory or memory fragment to focus on at a time.

3. Invite your adult self to meet your younger self.

Take your time to notice how it is for you as an adult to arrive there and be noticed by your younger self. Also pay attention to how it feels for your younger self to have your adult self enter the picture.

4. Use your imagination to unfold the story of your adult self supporting your younger self.

You might ask what your younger self needs or would have loved to have for support. You can have any conversation, such as enquiring into what your younger self might have come to believe about themselves. Sometimes our younger selves blame themselves for situations beyond their control or come to falsely believe there was something wrong with them. You might feel moved to share some soothing, encouraging words and perhaps imagine giving your younger self a hug or taking their hands as you connect with them in the memory. Be open to how your imagination unfolds your interaction. Remember, be patient and creative in how you approach your younger self to earn their trust and have them want to return with you into their future.

5. Plan to walk back to present time together

Let your younger self know that you want to walk them back to present time so your adult self can take care of them. Perhaps tell your younger self about how your life has turned out and what you have learned along the way. When you both are ready, hold hands and imagine your adult self walking your younger self back to present time.

6. Decide together where your younger self can live.

This is for their safekeeping and so your adult self can focus on their adult lives. Maybe your younger self can shrink to fit inside your heart or perhaps you feel drawn to paint a picture of you both together to keep somewhere meaningful. You could choose to dedicate an object – perhaps a small crystal or ornament that can be placed somewhere in your home or work space – as a reminder of your adult ability to take care of a younger part of yourself.

7. Pause to notice how you feel before returning to your day.

You are welcome to repeat the visualisation at another time to meet your younger self at different ages and stages of life, helping to free yourself from other memories that don't serve you well or bolster your sense of worth. Note, this visualisation can expose limiting beliefs about ourselves that might play into depression and anxiety, such as a belief that we are alone in our helplessness or a sense that danger is always there deep down inside us. But it can also guide us to realise that we can change these beliefs now and that we can step into our adult self as well as our inner child. While this does not change what happened to us, it can change how we view ourselves and the situations of our lives.

Exercise 12.10

Surprise me! A brief inner journey

Timing: 5–10 minutes

This visualisation is an opportunity for spontaneous inspiration and guidance. Be open-minded – there is no right or wrong, just what your mind spontaneously comes up with that might hold relevance for you. You are welcome to read the instructions one at a time and pause after each step to visualise what is suggested.

1. Take three slow, even and deep breaths to transition into the visualisation.

2. Imagine five descending stairs appearing in front of you.

3. In your mind, count backwards from five to zero as you imagine walking down the five steps to arrive at a closed door. Let your imagination picture what it looks like.

4. When you get to the door, notice the door and its handle, taking a moment to stand in front of it. Know that when you open it, you will be taken somewhere, like a dream, that you can become curious about.

5. When you feel ready, open the door. Look through and gain your first impression. When you are ready, step through. Where have you been taken? Allow the scene to unfold around you. Like a dream, the scene may change as you spend time there or it may stay the same.

6. Explore your surroundings, noticing sights, sounds, perhaps smells or the temperature of the air. What or who is around you? How do you feel in this space?

7. Find something that draws your attention and walk towards it. Study it for a few curious moments then ask, 'Do you have a message for me?' Allow this message to be delivered – perhaps it is told, felt or shown. Consider the relevance of this to some aspect of your life.

8. If there is a specific question you feel drawn to ask, you are welcome to do so. Be open to how it might be answered (sometimes with words or a sense of something or perhaps with a change of scenery). Again, you can consider how this is relevant to you. Remain in the visualisation and your curiosity about it for as long as feels good or engaging.

9. Before you leave, consider if there is anything you can take back with you to help you remember the experience, only if you are drawn to.

10. When ready, return to the door. When you reach it, decide how you wish to say goodbye to the experience, such as looking back one more time and saying thank you. Then step through and close the door behind you.

11. Walk up the five steps in front of you, counting from one to five.

12. Take three slow, deep breaths before opening your eyes if they were closed and transitioning back into your day. Carry with you the message or inspiration from the experience, or simply the momentary stilling of time and quieting of your mind that dipping into imagination can provide.

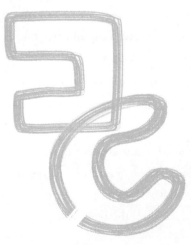

chapter 13

Sharpen mental clarity and grow inner joy with mindfulness

'If you are depressed you are living in the past. If you are anxious you are living in the future. If you are at peace you are living in the present.' — Lao Tzu

This chapter's stress toolkit:

Exercise 13.1   A mindfulness practice

indfulness, often cultivated through meditation, is all about honing present-moment awareness as well as sharpening our ability to focus on one thing at a time. There are many ways to invite focus into the moment. For example, some meditation practices guide attention to the observation of natural breathing, sensations in the body, observing nature, or repeating a mantra or phrase in our minds. The objective is to shift our attention away from the mindless inner chatter that keeps us living in the past or future, and towards direct experience of life in the here and now.

Mindfulness practice is best introduced when depression or anxiety symptoms are not at their worst. This is because distress can hinder our ability to learn new skills. For optimal learning, it is best to be in a relatively calm state. Once we are familiar with the practice, we can draw on it even when feeling distressed.

Benefits of mindfulness

Mindfulness can offer measurable benefits to the brain and body. Research has revealed how a regular meditation practice can:

- **Stimulate our ability to think more clearly** and logically and concentrate on what we choose, by increasing activity in the left prefrontal cortex. This can help with feeling more purposeful and in control. Higher activity in the right prefrontal cortex, conversely, is associated with a wandering, ruminating mind, which has been associated with greater negativity, anxiety and depression.

- **Improve integration and connectivity** between different parts of the brain towards more optimal functioning, such as the hippocampus and prefrontal cortex, to help with accessing our rational intelligence when faced with stress and stressful memories.

- **Improve memory, learning and ability to put experience into context.** This is due to the regrowth of neurons in the brain's hippocampus. Long-term depression and trauma undermine this, while a mindfulness practice has the potential to gradually reverse this when applied diligently.

- **Improve stress resilience and reduce reactivity.** When we use a mindfulness practice for 10–20 minutes daily for a few months, it can reduce the size and reactivity of the amygdala. The amygdala is like the brain's alarm system for danger; it can become enlarged and over-reactive with prolonged stress or trauma, making us more prone to acute stress responses such as fight, flight or collapse. With a mindfulness practice comes a more grounded outlook, better discernment between what is real and imagined, and a tendency to be more purposeful in our decision-making.

- **When an element of loving-kindness or compassion** is added to a meditation practice, research shows that this activates the brain areas associated with wanting to be of service to others and align with the greater good. Some areas of the brain also literally thicken from meditation practice, such as the insulae associated with qualities such as empathy and compassion. Along with this tends to come a more positive outlook as well as feeling more warmly connected with ourselves, others and our world.

Because of these kinds of benefits, mindfulness practice has been referred to as both a natural antidepressant and anxiolytic. It hones our relaxation response, and with fewer stress hormones coursing through us, can be excellent for both our mental and physical health.

Formal versus informal mindfulness practice

A formal practice means that you carve out time, like 5–20 minutes a day, to carry out your meditation of choice. This chapter offers you an accessible practice you can learn and use in this formal way.

You can also practise mindfulness informally to top up on present-moment awareness. Thich Nhat Hanh was a famous advocate of having an informal mindfulness practice woven through each day. His recommendations included doing one thing at a time and really focusing on it, such as eating, walking, or doing the dishes. He recommended to 'drink your tea slowly and reverently, as if it is the axis on which the earth revolves – slowly, evenly, without rushing towards the future. Live the actual moment. Only this moment is life.'

In his book, *Peace Is Every Step* he suggests setting up a breathing room or space in your home with a few simple items to help create a mindful mood, such as a candle, a comfortable seat to sit on, and a plant or flowers. Whenever you feel emotional or need some time to yourself, he says, go into this place and practise being with yourself and your feelings. You might do so by breathing slowly and attentively with and through your feelings as an emotion-mindfulness practice. This can train us to be more comfortable with and trusting of our emotions and their transient nature.

Exercise 13.1

A mindfulness practice

Timing: Allow about 5–20 minutes for this practice.

For this practice, imagine your attention as a flashlight, shining light on wherever you direct it to focus. With depression or anxiety, your thoughts, feelings and sensations might feel jumbled up inside you. This mindfulness practice invites you to differentiate aspects of your internal and external experience for the potentially organising and stress-relieving effects it can have. The practice invites you to move your attention sequentially between:

- thoughts
- feelings and emotions
- physical sensations
- breathing and heartbeat as experience of basic aliveness
- nature and the world outside us
- and back again.

Setting up for the practice

1. Read through the instructions and try to remember the focal points. Practise at a time of day that works for you.

2. Meditation is often practised with the eyes closed to avoid distraction, although if you are not comfortable to do this, you can rest your eyes softly on a focal point in front of you.

3. Sit comfortably upright, perhaps propped up by some cushions, sitting on a chair or the ground depending on your comfort.

4. Allow 5–30 minutes for this practice, depending on the time you have. The 5-minute option requires your familiarity with the practice, so at first allow at least 15 minutes to familiarise yourself with the process. You can set an alarm for the time you have.

5. Know that your mind will wander as you go along – expect it. Plan to return your attention to the task at hand with kindness each time your attention wanders. This is what builds your attention 'muscle' to hold attention in the present moment for longer stretches of time. Keep in mind that this is what meditation practice is designed to train you to do.

6. You can feel into how long you wish to spend with each step of the process before moving on to the next.

7. Always close with the final step of sending love outwards and back into yourself.

Undertaking the practice

1. Thoughts and mind

Spend a few moments noticing your thoughts, and whatever is or has been on your mind. Notice the quality of your thinking, such as thinking fast or sluggishly, feeling stuck or blocked for ideas, or having an easy flow of thoughts. Allow your thoughts and the storylines they tell to be there. You might notice how, at times, there are spaces between thoughts. Where does your mind go then?

There is a wide open field of inspiration and ideas that our minds can tune into in the spaces between thoughts. An image often used in mindfulness practices is that thoughts are like clouds passing through the clear blue sky of consciousness. Feel free to pay attention to both the clouds and the sky.

2. Feelings and emotions

Move your attention to your emotions or feelings. What kinds of feelings are with you now? Maybe you can name some emotions, such as anger, sadness or fear. Or you might simply be with feelings and notice where in your body you feel these feelings. Perhaps they are mainly in your chest, throat or gut area. Perhaps your feelings swirl, churn, flutter or sit inside these areas. Perhaps they feel hard, soft, fluttery, shivery, or tight.

Perhaps they feel light, open and heart-warming. Also observe how feelings rise up, last for a while then disappear; they never last forever.

Notice how feelings and emotions can follow your thoughts. They can be influenced by what is going on around you, in your relationships and your world. They also seem to have a mind of their own.

3. Body sensations

Turn your attention to your body. Can you notice where in your body you are feeling your feelings? Perhaps you spontaneously notice a part of your body for whatever reason, maybe an ache, pain or pleasant sensation. Take a few moments to see what areas call your attention.

Carry out a head-to-toe body scan to tune into more of your body as a whole. Spend a few moments with each part in turn, feeling for any sensations that might be obvious or subtle. Perhaps you can pick up on warmth, tingling or pulsing in some areas, or pressure, tension, tightness, fullness, numbness, emptiness or openness – whatever is there. Breathe gently into each area where your attention goes, to enliven it and help you focus on it more clearly.

4. Basic aliveness, breath breathing, heart beating

Now turn your attention to the natural ebb and flow of your breathing. Breathe through your nose if you can. You might notice how deeply your in-breath penetrates your body and how far out your out-breath flows into the space around you. Perhaps your in-breath is cooler than your out-breath because your body warms the breath you release.

Shift your attention to your heartbeat, listening, feeling or imagining feeling its rhythm. Feel or imagine how with each beat of your heart, there is a pulse of life through your body. Relaxing your body from head to fingers and toes can help you feel this more strongly. Spend a few moments with the experience of your heart determinedly beating, delivering vital nourishment to your body's cells.

Explore the possibility of focusing simultaneously on heartbeat and breathing, both representing aspects of your basic aliveness. It can be challenging at first to hold both in your awareness at the same time with their different rhythms, but it is possible with practice. It can feel like contacting the living, breathing bedrock of your human experience that exists beneath your thoughts, your feelings and what is going on in your life. Tuning into this basic level of our aliveness can feel subtly energising and refreshing.

5. Nature and the world outside you

Turn your attention to nature. Look out a window or perhaps you are sitting outside. Or recall natural places where you enjoy spending time, which might be filled with trees, plants, grass and flowers, forests, oceans, rocks, lakes, or mountains. Imagine the earth as rich soil for your feet to root in. Tune into all that lives in the biosphere around you, including birds, bees, bugs, frogs, lizards, butterflies and more. Imagine the vast, expansive sky above you, containing the sun, moon, stars and far-off universes. You could also tune into the day's weather, maybe with sunshine, clouds, wind or rain.

Follow wherever your mind takes you in the natural world. You might spend a few conscious moments breathing the air, absorbing its oxygenating nourishment and noticing how you are an interconnected part of nature. Does this awareness shift you in some way, perhaps growing your peace of mind?

6. Reverse the process from sensations up to thinking

Start with nature where your attention has just been. Move into awareness of basic aliveness with breath breathing and heart beating, then into body awareness of sensations. Perhaps do a reverse body scan, from toes to your head, gently breathing into each part in turn. Move your attention onto your emotions or feelings, and finally up to your thinking or clear mind.

Your experience while reversing the process may feel different from when you started out with the exercise. Do you notice anything different now in your feeling tone or state of mind? When you are ready, close with the final step of 'sending love' (step 8) or if you wish you can repeat the process before closing.

7. Repeat the process

You can repeat the process as many times as you like, such as three to five times of moving awareness between each of these touchpoints for a longer meditation practice. Or you can practise for a particular amount of time, rather than counting the times you repeat the process. It can be helpful to set a gentle alarm, such as for 10–20 minutes and allow a minute or two extra to conclude with step 8 of 'sending love'. Whether timed or counting rounds through the practice, you can experiment with moving more slowly and more quickly through the stages for some variation.

8. Sending love outwards and back to yourself

No matter how many times you repeated the steps, close your practice with this touch of heartfelt compassion:

- Call to mind someone or something that truly warms your heart. It could be the laugh of a baby, the cuteness of a young animal or the face of a loved one. Notice how pleasant feelings can rise up to fill you; as much as you can, allow them to spread outwards from your heart through your body and perhaps into the space around you.

- Send this warmth or love from your heart, outwards into the world in general or towards the image of someone who might need it. You are welcome to add your own wish or prayer for the well-being of others.

- Circle your warmth back to surround yourself with this same loving care for a few nourishing moments. If you wish, say a prayer or send a wish to yourself, such as to ease any suffering. Or simply bask in the sense of being surrounded with love.

- When you are ready, mark the close of your practice with a deep breath and a body stretch before opening your eyes if they were shut and returning to your day or night.

Some closing inspiration from trauma resolution expert Peter Levine, *In an Unspoken Voice* (p. 182):

'With a little practice we can . . . separate out emotions, thoughts and beliefs from the underlying sensations. We [can then be] astounded by our capacity to tolerate and pass through difficult emotional states, such as terror, rage and helplessness, without being swept away and drowned. If we go "underneath" the overwhelming emotions and touch into physical sensations, something quite profound occurs in our organism – there is a sense of flow, of "coming home".'

chapter 14

Movement sequence for releasing tension and replenishing energy

'Nature does not hurry yet everything is accomplished.' **— Lao Tzu**

This chapter's stress toolkit:

Exercise 14.1   Movement sequence for releasing tension and replenishing energy

 ovement that is slow, smooth and graceful stimulates our relaxation response and can relieve tension. In contrast, movements that are jerky, forceful or quick tend to stimulate our stress responses. This chapter offers a movement sequence designed to increase your sense of flow, physical ease and grace while promoting a clearer and more positive outlook. It draws on the age-old mindful movement practice of qigong that dates back thousands of years as an effective support for physical and mental health. For those who do not appreciate a sitting meditation practice, this can provide a mindful movement alternative that has stood the test of time and now enjoys ample scientific backing.

You can use this movement sequence first thing in the morning or in a break in your day for releasing tension and replenishing energy. It is an excellent way to deepen your relaxation response through movement. The movements naturally guide you to slow down your breathing so you enter resonance frequency breathing (see Chapter 5) of 5–10 breaths per minute, in contrast to the average 12–20 breaths per minute. This can induce a state of relaxation that can feel deeply nourishing, soothing for anxiety and subtly uplifting from depression.

Timing: 15–20 minutes (can be extended for longer if you wish by repeating the movements)

The movement sequence:

- starts with a warm-up involving a series of tension-relieving movements such as shaking out, twisting and tapping the body. This is followed by a series of slow movements coordinated with breathing. The outcome can be that your whole body feels more integrated in a way that feels satisfying and improves body awareness and balance.

- slows down your breathing. Unless otherwise specified, breathing for all the movements is recommended to be in through your nose if you can, and out through either the nose or mouth according to your preference.

- is intended as a standing sequence. If you are not able to stand, you can adapt the movements to a sitting position in your way. If sitting, simply use the arm movements and adapt movements to a sitting position as best you can.

The movements are designed to be accessible for most levels of physical ability and fitness. You are invited to adapt movements to work around any physical limitations. Never push yourself beyond your level of comfort, remembering that the main intention is to de-stress and slow down to boost your sense of well-being, grounding, stress resilience and optimism.

Exercise 14.1

Movement sequence for releasing tension and replenishing energy

Timing: Allow about 15–20 minutes for this practice.

1. Getting started

- **Stand tall with feet and legs together** and arms comfortably at your sides. Lengthen your posture, rising to your full height and standing tall between earth and sky.
- **Bring hands into a prayer pose** at your chest and take a deep breath as a gesture of coming into the moment. Then return arms to your sides.

2. Step one foot out to the side to stand with feet hip distance (or a comfortable distance) apart

- **Feet are parallel with knees soft or slightly bent,** so you feel well grounded through your feet. This will be your standing position for all the following exercises unless otherwise specified.

3. Loosen your neck

- **Draw a figure-8 in the air in front of you,** led by your nose, in one direction then the other. The intention is to loosen up your neck with smaller or bigger circles, depending on your comfort and range of motion. Be mindful not to hurt your neck.

- **Carry out three slow figure-8s** in one direction then the other. When at the highest point with your nose, be mindful to keep your spine long and reach your nose upwards to avoid crunching into the back of your neck. Follow what feels easy, satisfying and mobilising for this area.

4. Shake out

- **Arms and hands.** Shake out your arms and hands for a few moments (in whatever way feels good). You can play with raising and lowering your arms as you shake off tension through the hands and fingers.

- **Shoulders and hips.** Shake out shoulders and hips together, however feels organic. This can loosen up your whole torso and spine. Let your legs and arms jiggle along with the shaking movements while keeping your feet grounded and stable in their standing position.

5. Twist and tap

Make your hands into soft fists and begin a twisting motion from side to side, allowing your arms to swing outwards. Wrap them around your torso naturally as you look over the shoulder of the side you are twisting towards. Keep knees slightly bent throughout and feet stable and grounded. Tap your body at two levels:

- **Tap at mid-abdomen level.** Arms wrap around the waist with fists tapping wherever they land naturally, one hand in front (front of fist making contact) and one behind (back of fist making contact), depending on which side you are turning to. The head turns from side to side in the direction of your twist. Breathe out in a short burst (out of nose or mouth) each time you tap on your body so your breathing will be relatively quick following the swinging motion. You can imagine breathing out tension each exhalation. Swing 16 times (eight each side) or as much as feels good.

- **Tap on the top corner of your chest.** Arms again swing around your body as the torso and head twist from side to side. This time, raise your front arm a little higher so the front fist taps on the front upper corner of your chest in the soft indent below your collarbone. The back hand simply swings around to tap on your lower back wherever it naturally reaches, with the back of your hand making contact with your lower back. Again, breathe out in a short bursts each time you tap so breathing is relatively quick following the swinging motion. Repeat to a mental count of 16 or as feels good.

Slow down your swinging to come to a standstill. Knees remain slightly bent.

6. Bounce into bent legs

- **Play with bouncing into your bent legs** to release tension downwards into the ground. Imagine your body following the bouncing motion as if it were a rag doll. Feet remain flat on the ground throughout. Continue for as long as feels good, allowing your body to loosen up and follow the bouncing motion naturally.

- **To bring the bouncing to an end,** press down into your feet and rise up into a standing position with knees soft and spine reaching upwards towards the sky in a way that feels comfortable and uplifting.

7. Open and close your arms like a bird's wings

Bend into your knees as much as feels comfortable, keeping your posture upright and avoiding leaning forwards. Start with arms relaxed at your sides.

- **Breathe in while raising arms up at your sides** with palms down (like opening your wide open wings). As you do so, extend your legs by pressing down through your feet as you stand taller.

- **Breathe out while slowly lowering your arms down to your sides,** bending into your knees as much as feels comfortable with feet remaining flat on the ground.

- **Repeat three to nine times,** slowing down movement and breathing as much as you can. Aim for about 4 or 5 seconds per in-breath and the same per out-breath.

Notes: Coordinate breath and movement with arms and legs reaching their highest position at the end of your inhalation and their lowest position at the end of your exhalation.

If your shoulders limit your movement, only raise your arms as much as you can or raise them forwards if easier.

Avoid hiking up your shoulders on inhalation by keeping them relaxed and having a good space between shoulders and ears.

Breathe in and out from your belly to avoid upper-chest breathing and increase a sense of grounding. To further encourage this, you might imagine inhalations starting from the ground and moving up through feet and body, and exhalations descending through your body and feet to end in the ground beneath you.

8. Calming air shower

This is a version of an age-old practice for symbolically showering ourselves with air, and the universal life force believed to be carried in air, for soothing effect. The 'air shower' is facilitated by the movement of your arms, which can feel like drawing air and a sense of calmness down through your body.

- **Start with arms at sides and knees comfortably bent** (feet flat on the ground).

- **Inhale, coordinating breath and movement** as you raise the arms sideways and up overhead while extending the legs as follows:
  - **Arms**. Turn palms outwards and raise arms sideways and overhead as if scooping air upwards. When the arms arrive overhead, allow them to round and form a circle framing your face, with palms facing down and shoulders relaxed.
  - **Legs.** As you raise your arms overhead, allow your legs to straighten so you stand taller.

- **Exhale, coordinating breath and movement** as you lower the arms in front of your body and bend comfortably into your legs again as follows:
  - **Arms.** With palms facing downwards and fingertips a small distance apart, slowly lower your hands downwards in front of you, as if drawing air downwards through your body to calm yourself from top to toe (even though your arms only reach as far as your hips and you need to imagine the calm extending down to your toes). At the end of this movement, hands are in front of your hips with palms facing the ground and fingertips pointing in towards each other.
  - **Legs.** As you lower your arms in front of you, bend into your knees to return to the starting position with feet remaining flat on the ground, while feeling well grounded through your feet.

- **When hands are at their lowest position,** rotate arms outwards so the palms face outwards again at your sides. Repeat the air scooping and showering movements. Scoop air upwards and overhead on inhalation, and press air downwards in front of your body on exhalation.

- **Repeat three to nine times, slowing down the flow of breathing** and movement as much as feels comfortable, and maintaining a smooth and continuous flow of breathing and movement. To further enhance the relaxing effect, extend exhalations to be longer than inhalations, such as breathing in for a mental count of four or five, and breathing out for a mental count of six to eight.

- **End by relaxing arms at sides.**

> **Note:** If you suffer from low blood pressure or are prone to feeling light-headed, you can reverse the leg bending and extending so the legs bend as you inhale raising arms overhead, and straighten as you exhale bringing arms downwards in front of you. This can increase a stabilising effect of this movement as opposed to emphasising calming down, which can lower blood pressure. Your head rises upwards as the arms descend, which can give a feeling of standing taller and symbolically rising above or growing through challenges.

9. Reach to the sky

- **With arms at your sides, bring your feet together** and extend your legs to stand tall. Feet remain flat on the ground with knees soft (not locking) to feel the ground beneath your feet.

- **Breathe in and reach arms sideways and up** as in the previous exercise, but this time meet your hands overhead in a prayer pose that reaches up towards the sky. If your shoulder range is limited, you can meet hands in a prayer pose at a level that works for you, such as in front of your chest. Head remains looking forwards.

- **At the top of your inhalation,** raise your heels slightly off the ground for an upwards stretch of your body. Find your balance there for a moment. If arms are at chest level, simply lengthen your spine and reach upwards through the crown of your head as you raise your heels.

- **Exhale, returning heels to the ground** while slowly bringing your prayer pose down to chest level. Take a deep breath in this position.

- **End by bringing hands down to cover your lower belly** (just below your navel) with one hand on top of the other. Take a deep breath into this area.

10. Belly and chest massage

- **Massage your belly in circles in a clockwise direction** that follows your digestion, keeping hands one on top of the other and flat on your belly. Massage in bigger and smaller circles around your navel, as feels good and for as long as you like, perhaps drawing three to nine circles to massage your whole abdominal area.

- **Move your right hand to the centre of your chest,** with left hand remaining on your lower belly. Rub in circles over the centre of your chest as many times as feels good and soothing, perhaps three to nine times. Then switch hands to rub the centre of your chest with your left hand a few times.

- **Bring one hand on top of the other at the centre of your chest.** Press them for a transitional moment before the following exercise.

11. Heart clearing and opening

- **Step into a wider stance again** with your feet parallel and knees slightly bent.

- **Bring hands into a prayer pose at chest level** then part your hands slightly in this position as you take a deep breath in.

- **Breathe out, extending arms forwards and out to your sides** at about shoulder height with hands pressing forwards and outwards as if pushing something away. (Fingers point upwards.)

- **Breathe in, reversing the path** so hands return to a slightly parted prayer pose at chest level.

- **Repeat three to nine times, coordinating breath with movement.** As you go along, you can imagine releasing any hurts from your heart with your out-breath, and taking in healthy resources and energy from the atmosphere with your in-breaths. Then visualise giving out good energy from your heart into the world on your out-breaths, and receiving goodness on your in-breaths.

This movement can also feel like a practice for setting healthy boundaries through our hands delineating personal space, as well as potentially boosting a sense of personal strength in a way that emanates from the heart.

12. Full body sweep

- **Start with hands in a prayer pose at chest level** and rub them together for a few warming moments before starting the body sweep. This will run overhead, down the back of your body and up the front a few times for subtly energising effect.

- **Bring your hands to cup over your eyes** then brush hands over your forehead and head and down the back of your neck, circling around your shoulders and down the sides of your torso to arrive with hands placed on your lower back.

- **Give your lower back a rub** to warm this area for a few moments. This can help us to feel warmer and safer from the inside out. Then take a deep breath in.

- **Breathe out, brushing hands down the backs of your legs** and around the outsides of your feet, bending your knees, lowering your head and rounding your spine as you go to allow for reaching down towards your feet. If you cannot reach all the way, keep hands in contact with legs as long as you can and imagine drawing a circle in the air around your feet to complete the movement.

- **Breathe in, brushing hands around the insides of your feet and up the insides of your legs,** continuing to sweep hands upwards over the front of your hips to come together in a prayer pose at chest level. Allow legs to straighten (knees remain soft) as you unfold your spine to upright with head coming up last. If you cannot reach to your feet, simply make contact with your legs at the level that you are able to complete the movement.

- **Repeat three times, always starting by rubbing your hands together** before cupping your eyes and sweeping overhead, round to your lower back for a brief rub, then down the backs of your legs, up the front of your legs and back to prayer pose at chest level.

13. Paint an imaginary rainbow around yourself

- **Start in the prayer pose.**

- **Inhale, raising hands above your head** (or as high as you can) while separating hands so the palms face upwards and fingers point towards each other. Arms are rounded and framing your head. At the top of your inhalation, press palms upwards to the sky so arms extend.

- **Exhale, circling arms sideways and down** as you imagine your hands painting a rainbow around yourself to frame your body in this colourful, potentially uplifting way. When your arms have completed the circle, meet hands in front of hips and raise them up to return to prayer pose at chest level.

- **Repeat three times, smiling** to enhance the beauty of the image of painting a colourful, protective boundary around yourself. End with arms in a prayer pose at chest level and take a deep breath.

14. Closing movements

- **Step your feet together into a comfortable standing position,** keeping hands in a prayer pose.
- **Take a deep breath in and bow as you exhale** to mark the end of the sequence.
- **Add a touch of gratitude and compassion** while holding hands in prayer pose and standing tall. You might say a prayer or send a wish in your mind to yourself and anyone else who might need it. You can also extend heartfelt warmth as far outwards as feels good, such as to the far reaches of our world and to all living beings, wishing for the well-being of all. You might also notice the heartfelt strength this can build in you. Imagine circling warmth back to yourself so you can feel warmly centred in yourself before closing the movement practice.

15. Optional extra to get you going again – a brief walking meditation

This can be a mindful way to transition out of the movement sequence into your day. It involves a minute or two of mindful walking (or longer if you like), which means walking slowly enough to notice the details of weight change and foot placement on the ground with each step. This can extend to greater mindfulness and balance in your natural walking thereafter. After carrying out the walking practice, you might be surprised at how much tension you might carry in habitual walking. This walking meditation can remind you to let go of unnecessary tension or rushing, towards moving through your day in a more relaxed, yet focused way. Practising even a few mindful steps or for a minute or so after the movement sequence can have this effect.

You can adapt this mindful walking to any way you might move about your day. For example, if you have an injury, a physical anomaly or move about in a wheelchair, you can apply the mindful 'walking' by slowing your unique way of moving so you can more closely observe how you go about it, while potentially improving balance and releasing unnecessary tension.

How to go about it

- **Stand with legs hip-distance apart** in a comfortable stance with knees soft so you can feel the ground beneath your feet. Arms are relaxed at your sides.

- **Walk very slowly so you can feel the transition from one foot to the other** and how your weight shifts in the process. Feel the ground beneath your foot as you place it down. Each time you place a foot on the ground, find your balance and stability over that foot before taking your next step. You might imagine the leg you are standing into is 'full' because it carries all your weight and the other leg is 'empty' because it is free and ready to take the next step. This can help you become more mindful of how you place your feet on the ground and can improve your balance over time.

- **Play with taking slow and mindful steps around your space.** You are welcome to play with walking forwards, backwards or around in a circle, as you wish. You can also add a slow sense of flow to your walking to make it smooth and continuous.

- **End with legs in a comfortable standing position** with knees relaxed to feel well grounded before moving at your usual speed into the rest of your day.

chapter 15

STEPS for goal-setting, problem-solving and personal growth

'Focus on your goals, not your fear.' — **Roy Bennett**

This chapter's stress toolkit:

Exercise 15.1 STEPS for goal-setting, problem-solving and personal growth

his chapter offers a model to inspire proactive goal-setting, problem-solving and personal growth around the acronym STEPS. It is designed to guide your thinking from where you are now to where you would like to be, as well as planning towards your goal with achievable practical steps, no matter how small they may be. The intention is to encourage regular investment in positive, proactive progress to help guide your life in meaningful directions. This can boost your motivation and a sense of accomplishment to counteract depression. It can also ease anxiety by helping to clear your mind and encourage proactivity.

The STEPS process can be used on a need-for basis or regularly, depending on your preference. While it is recommended as a written exercise, you are welcome to talk it through with a supportive person. Initially, you'll want to set aside about 20–30 minutes to thoroughly think through your longer- and shorter-term goals and action plans. Then if you are revisiting goals or refreshing action steps, the process can be relatively quick (such as in 10 minutes).

The STEPS acronym

S – Situation now

What is something you would like or need to focus on now? It could be any aspect of life, such as physical or mental health, happiness, career or work, or relationships. Reflect on a current challenge affecting you or an aspect of your life. Or consider what may be playing into the situation that may be causing it or keeping it in place.

Sometimes a challenge is like an iceberg. Initially, we might be aware of the tip of the iceberg of our thoughts, feelings or things playing into a situation. As we ask ourselves what else might be playing into it, more of the iceberg that lies beneath the surface can be exposed. Playing a part could be a personal attitude, the actions of others, an event in our community or world, or some big life crisis. The more layers we uncover, the more effectively we can identify solutions that target these layers towards resolution and personal growth.

T – To where?

What is a positive outcome to your current situation? This could be your hopes, dreams, goals and aspirations for the short and long term. Having goals that inspire us and a way to think through and plan towards them can be energising – increasing our motivation to want to achieve them.

Initially, our goals or aspirations might be less clear than they could be. Some thought towards clarifying details could be helpful and can be a creative thinking process in itself. This step is a great opportunity to visualise your future self and best possible outcomes for inspiration, for which the visualisations in Chapter 12 can be helpful.

Your goals can also change and evolve over time, so whenever you revisit the STEPS process, pause and reflect on whether your goals need some refreshing or updating so they can stay relevant and compelling.

E – Everything you could do

How can you go from where you are now to where you would like to be? Free and wild brainstorming is encouraged here to explore as many options as possible, from which you can then choose in the next stage of the process. Thinking outside the box is encouraged, such as to come up with five ideas rather than just one or two. You might write in point form or a list, or use a mind map with lots of branches to invite lots of possible options for addressing different aspects of your situation.

This is an invitation to dig deeply into creative thinking and maybe bounce ideas off someone who will listen and add their input. You can dissect your goals into component parts so you can more clearly see the steps to take to achieve your goals. For example, you might want to achieve a better work–life balance. On closer inspection, maybe you can take better care of your mental health by exercising regularly, allocating more time for cooking, enjoying more time with friends and family, and being more productive during your work hours.

Consider ideas for how you might go about achieving these things. The next step is to choose the most accessible or highest priority ideas and organise them into a plan of action.

P and S – Plan of action that is Specific

This is where you get to choose from the 'everything you could do' options and commit to taking specific actions. The 'I did it' sense of accomplishment that can come from accomplishing even the smallest thing can then boost motivation to keep going.

For this reason, try choosing actions that are achievable. You might pick one or two of the options from the previous step, and describe how and by when you plan to accomplish them. It could involve an action for the day or week, or a set of tasks for the month – it's up to you what feels realistic.

Remember to prioritise and address the highest priorities at the time. Then encourage yourself to return to the STEPS over time to refresh your progress. Your action steps can include a commitment to carry out an exercise from this book, or perhaps call a friend or family member for support. It could be a plan to include something playful or enjoyable in your week, or focus on work-based tasks or steps towards a new business idea. There is no limit to what you could choose to focus on, so long as you are investing in your forward movement in meaningful and constructive ways.

Exercise 15.1

STEPS for goal-setting, problem-solving and personal growth

Timing: Allow about 10–30 minutes for this written exercise.

Preparation

You will need a piece of paper. Divide the page into four quadrants by drawing a cross through the centre of the page. Dedicate one quadrant to each stage of the STEPS acronym. Or you could use four pieces of paper and dedicate one page to each of the four STEPS.

Getting started

Maybe you start with a problem or challenge that you're facing, or with a goal you want to achieve. You are welcome to cycle between each of the stages of the STEPS process many times as you progress your thinking, letting new ideas come up. Generally, you would write in the 'PS' section last because then you can prioritise your specific plan of action based on all you have identified.

Sometimes a plan of action is clear early on in the process. In this case, you can write it in to commit to it then you are welcome to add to it as you go along with other action ideas that are important at the time.

Sample questions to guide your thinking

Each STEP is an opportunity for reflection. The more deeply we think about our challenges, the more effective our problem-solving tends to be. Then we can shift from knee-jerk reactivity to conscious proactivity.

Following are some questions to stimulate your thinking. You do not have to run through all of them. Perhaps get your mind going with a few of them. You are welcome to use as many as you like, or even add to the list by making up your own, as you delve more deeply into the matter at hand and what you could do to address it. It can also be helpful to have a thinking partner or friend, who can ask you some of these questions and possibly expand your thinking with their feedback and ideas.

Sample STEPS questions

S	T
Situation now	**To where?**
What is a challenge or issue you would like or need to focus on now?	What would you like to achieve or see happen?
What thoughts, feelings and behaviours might be linked to this situation?	You might include goals, dreams, hopes and aspirations.
How is the situation affecting different aspects of your life, such as personally and professionally?	What would success look and feel like?
What feedback have you received about it?	What might your goal be in the short term?
What have you tried so far and how did that go?	What might your goal be in the long term?
Are there any assumptions to be checked?	If you had a magic wand to turn the situation around, and anything were possible, what would the outcome be?
What might be playing a part in this situation?	You can also refer to the visualisations for 'Your best future self' in Chapter 12 to further guide your thinking (see exercises 12.7 and 12.8).
What else might be playing into my situation now? In this, you can consider what might lie beneath the obvious that might keep the situation in place inside yourself, with others or events beyond your control. The more clearly you identify these influencing factors, the more effectively you can problem-solve by addressing each of them.	

E	PS
Everything you could do	Plan of action that is Specific
How could you begin to move towards your goals or aspirations?	What are you willing to commit to doing and by when?
Come up with at least five different options, being as creative as you can, trying to think outside the box.	What feels like the highest priority action right now that you want or need to attend to?
How do you feel about the options so far?	What are possible obstacles you might encounter and ideas to overcome them?
If you could change just one thing, what would that be and how could you go about it?	Would you like to prioritise other action items for future reference? When might you accomplish them? These can be brought forward into the next STEPS process.
What are the outcomes of some of those options? This allows you to consider different scenarios.	
What else might be possible?	What support might you need or would be helpful and from whom?
What advice would you give to a friend in your situation?	When do you plan to return to the STEPS process to update and refresh the information based on your progress and what has transpired?
Have you thought of ideas for addressing all aspects that might be playing into your situation?	

Part 4

Concluding thoughts
and inspiration

chapter 16

Building a lasting sense of stress mastery

'Freedom is a lifetime practice –
a choice we get to make again and again
each day ... Ultimately freedom requires
hope, which I define in two ways: the
awareness that suffering, however terrible,
is temporary and the curiosity to discover
what happens next.' — **Edith Eger, in** *The Gift*

This chapter's stress toolkit:

Exercise 16.1   Keeping your practice fresh and Interesting

Exercise 16.2   Making the most of positive moments

Exercise 16.3   Tracking your progress with relapse prevention in mind

- Reflections on staying connected with your social circles
- Levels of stress interest, awareness and mastery – what to aspire towards

ou've been on a journey to arrive at this final chapter. Maybe you have read or skimmed through the book. Maybe you have tried some of the practices or flagged a few that seem interesting for delving into later. How you have arrived here is less important than what you do from here on forwards.

Three questions for you in this final chapter are:

1. How can you turn temporary exploration into a lasting sense of stress mastery?

2. How can you turn 'ah-ha' moments or passing fascination into something that sticks?

3. What does it take to keep motivated to achieve the long-term outcomes you might wish for?

Research is clear that you need repetition over a period of time for lasting change. This could be practising what interests you most for a period of time. You might try out a short practice once or twice a day for a few days in a row to feel what it offers you. Or you could apply the classic 21 days to focus on certain techniques, maybe once or twice a day, so you can have more time to integrate learning and personal growth into longer-term memory. And sometimes our good intentions to keep up a practice are not enough. We might find ourselves losing interest, forgetting or having the practice start to feel like a burden. How can we then draw ourselves back to investing in ourselves?

Exercise 16.1

Keeping your practice fresh and interesting

Our human nature tends to need some help along the way to keep us moving in meaningful directions. Sometimes, for deeper healing or trauma resolution, we need the skilful guidance of a mental health professional to free us to continue to learn and grow. If this feels true for you, please seek out the support you need while also feeling free to use this book's toolkits to bolster you. Some of us may be open to personal learning and growth, but might struggle to stay focused on particular practices. Regardless of what each of our possible resistances or stumbling blocks are, some helpful strategies can keep us on a good track.

Here are some ways to spark interest and motivation when you might need it towards reaping maximum rewards on your stress-mastery journey:

Interest and curiosity

Follow the practices that interest you and pique your curiosity. Then your motivation will be right there with you. And when your interest and curiosity wanes, find what interests you next.

Novelty

This is an invitation to change it up when your interest wanes. Our brains wake up with novel experiences. This is because we are wired to be more alert and attentive when something feels new, just as we might be more attentive when on holiday in a new place. Some of us might not like the idea of change, or be daunted by it. In that case, you could apply novelty in smaller ways, such as experimenting with a new technique that feels accessible to you. If you tend to be an over-thinker, start with the mind toolkits and when you feel ready, try a body-based intervention too. You might be surprised by the results. The choice is yours.

An attitude of playfulness, adventure or experimentation

Play is a marvellous way to capture our attention. With playfulness, our brains are most receptive to learning. This could be because when we play, we are in the moment, having fun and less likely to be distracted by our thoughts. How can we bring an attitude of playfulness, adventure or experimentation into the opportunities offered in this book?

Here are some ideas:

1. **When trying out a new practice, take the pressure out of it**, removing the intention to achieve a particular outcome. Instead, treat it as a curious experiment or an adventure that your senses, mind or body are taken on.

2. **Keep an open mind** like a playful scientist carrying out research while trying out new techniques. This is in line with what Albert Einstein once said: 'Play is the highest form of research.'

3. **You might think of your progress as a game of snakes and ladders.** When you are uplifted, you can picture yourself climbing up a ladder and perhaps reaching new mental health heights. Or if anxiety, depression or an acute stress response has taken you for a slippery ride down a snake, you may be encouraged to throw the dice again to keep on keeping on. This might mean trying out a new practice or using one you know and like to help you progress again.

4. **If you are new to using body-based practices,** you could allow yourself to be entertained by how silly you feel at first in being asked to shake out or pandiculate your body (see Exercise 6.6). But you can have fun with it – perhaps feel like a child again as you explore the movements. If it makes you laugh, you are on a good track because laughing releases a gush of feel-good hormones that counteract anxiety and depression. Loosening up physically and letting ourselves laugh can be just what is needed for upliftment at the time. Of course, also be open to how you feel after you try out movements that feel silly at first but might later surprise you by how they make you feel.

5. **Design your own course to follow, using this book's toolkits.** This can let you progress in your own time. You might dedicate a few months to working through the book chapter by chapter, or choose to delve into particular aspects of the toolkits. You can treat it like a grand adventure that you are taking your mind and body on, filled with lots of opportunities to experiment and discover new experiences.

6. **You can gamify the process.** Perhaps allocate a point system for yourself: earning a point for each exercise you try in this book or a point over a month for every day you try a practice. You might also compete with a friend who is interested in the process to motivate each other. Make a time to speak about what you liked and did not like, and what is working best for each of you and how you might reward your progress.

7. **Surprise me!** Open the book on a random page and see what is there – it might hold a relevant message for you for the day. Try out something for no other reason than that you opened to it. There is also a visualisation practice in Chapter 12 called 'Surprise me' that you can try out if you feel ready for some spontaneous inner guidance and inspiration.

Exercise 16.2

Making the most of positive moments

An 'ah-ha' moment can be a turning point that inspires fresh insight and perspective. Or we could find ourselves basking in the glow of feeling really good, perhaps following one of the practices in this book, accomplishing something, or just spontaneously as we move through our days.

So that these moments can influence your stress resilience to a greater extent, one simple suggestion with scientific backing is to extend how much time you focus on your positive experiences each time you notice them. You might aim to add even 5 or 10 more seconds onto your feel-good moments. This allows your brain to register the experience and form new neural pathways towards remembering and recognising these positive experiences in future.

To do so, you could notice where in your body you feel the good feelings, or pause to breathe the good feelings through your body. Perhaps imagine them penetrating your body more deeply from head to toe with each breath. An example of a helpful study on this topic was carried out by psychologist Rick Hanson and colleagues at the University of California, Berkeley. It is all about learning to learn and maximise learning from positive experiences.

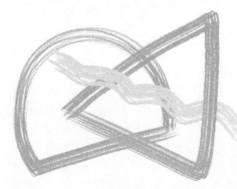

Exercise 16.3

Tracking your progress with relapse prevention in mind

It can be helpful to keep a journal or computer file to take and save notes about exercises you try out, how they worked for you and what your favourites are. This can give you something tangible to refer back to when anxiety or depression might visit again.

Staying connected with your social circles

This book is not about relationships specifically. All the practices can enrich our relationships through their invitation to live with greater presence and attentiveness to who and what matters to us. Connecting, face-to-face or over the phone, with the people in our lives can act like an antidepressant and anxiolytic.

Remember to play, go for walks, make time for deep conversations, talk through your worries, share your excitements, support those less fortunate than you, or any way you might choose to invest in each other. The mutual benefits can keep all of our nervous systems radiant with a sense of connection, care and belonging.

Remember, too, that relationships can be a cause of stress. Relationship research, such as by Edward Tronick and Andrew Gianano, finds that what makes relationships healthy and trusting is not whether they cause stress at times, but that there is mutual willingness to return and repair connection as soon as possible after discord. This might involve owning our part in a dynamic, apologising if need be, and being open to exploring how to do things differently in future. The tools in this book can encourage a frame of mind that supports relationship resilience.

Levels of stress interest, awareness and mastery – what to aspire towards

Here is a simple way to assess where you are in terms of stress management, and point to what you can aspire towards. This applies whether you consider yourself to be a beginner or advanced in the art of stress management. It is not about how many tools you have accumulated; rather, it is the depth of your experience with your chosen tools and the integration of these tools in your life.

What level are you on?

1. Mild or idle curiosity:

'I don't really need help, or don't have much time to spare, but I will learn some tricks and tips anyway, when I can.'

For you, stress management is a low-to-medium priority. This can range from not being aware of stress to knowing we are stressed, but not having or making much time to deal with it. Urgency is low and there might be a feeling of coping or needing to soldier on. Automatic stress reactivity is at play sometimes without much conscious awareness. There can be curiosity, perhaps idle or mild or even strong, but learning more about stress and trying out stress-management tools are deferred until later. Even as a sideline interest, experimenting with stress tools can be beneficial. It can also go on to pique our interest, encourage us to practise more, or at least know where to find this kind of support when we are ready.

2. High motivation or urgent need:

'I need help or I am hungry for this knowledge and I am sincerely trying some of the tools to discover what works well for me.'

For you, stress management is a high priority. Perhaps you are unable to ignore stress any longer and choose to do something about it, or you urgently need to ease stress in a crisis. In the heat of the moment, your ability to learn new things is limited. But if you use crises to propel your personal growth, then it can lead to a focused period of investing in stress-management practices. Then your stress toolkit can grow in leaps and bounds. Or sometimes, a new stage of life or curiosity to open to life in new ways can be what fires up your motivation to learn new things.

3. Integrated in life:

'I have a set of tools that work for me, which I draw on regularly or when I need to. I also enjoy trying out new stress tools when I feel like something fresh and new.'

Ultimately, this is what we are aspiring towards. Our stress toolkit serves us best in the long term when seamlessly integrated into our lives, which can take time and practice. For some of us, our journey started many years back, and for others, this is all very new. No matter where you find yourself, know you are gaining invaluable life skills to ease, enrich and empower how you navigate life. This journey works best when travelled at your own pace and in a way that feels true.

In the words of a tennis legend, Arthur Ashe:
'Start where you are, use what you have, do what you can.'

Even one tool well learned can make a world of difference.

Bibliography

American Psychiatric Association. (2013). *Diagnostic and statistical manual of mental disorders* (5th edition). Washington, D.C.: American Psychiatric Publishing.

Anderson, D.E., McNeely, J.D., Chesney, M.A., & Windham, B.G. (2008). Breathing variability at rest is positively associated with 24-h blood pressure level. *American Journal of Hypertension, 21*(12), 1324–1329. DOI:10.1038/ajh.2008.292

Anderson, D.E., & Chesney, M.A. (2002). Gender-specific association of perceived stress and inhibited breathing pattern. *International Journal of Behavioral Medicine (special issue), 9*(3), 216–217. DOI:10.1207/s15327558ijbm0903_04

Baikie, K., & Wilhelm, K. (2005). Emotional and physical health benefits of expressive writing. *Advances in Psychiatric Treatment, 11*(5), 338–346. doi:10.1192/apt.11.5.338

Benson, H., & Klipper, M.Z. (1975). *The relaxation response.* William Morrow & Co.: New York.

Bohr, C., Hasselbalch, K., & Krogh., A. (1904). Concerning a biologically important relationship – the influence of the carbon dioxide content of blood on its oxygen binding. In *Scandinavian Society for Physiology, 16*, 401–412.

Carillo, A., Rubio-Aparicio, M., Molinari, G., Enrique, Á., Sánchez-Meca, J., & Baños, R.M. (2019). Effects of the best possible self intervention: a systematic review and meta-analysis. *PloS One, 14*(9), e0222386. https://doi.org/10.1371/journal.pone.0222386

Chia, M. (2022). Alchemize your emotional energy for self-healing and longevity. The shift network. Retrieved December 2022 from https://theshiftnetwork.com/course/01MChia01_21

Chödrön, P. (2001). *Tonglen: The path of transformation.* Shambhala Media: Boulder, CO.

Cohen, K.S. (1997). *The way of qigong: The art and science of Chinese energy healing.* Ballantine Books: New York.

Dana, D., & Porges, S.W. (2018). *The polyvagal theory in therapy: Engaging the rhythm of regulation.* W.W. Norton & Company: New York.

Davidson, R.J. (n.d.). *Richard J. Davidson.* Retrieved December 2022 from https://www.richardjdavidson.com

Drogin, I. (2020). How to cultivate health and vitality with the microcosmic orbit. *Holden Qigong.* Retrieved December 2022 from https://www.holdenqigong.com/how-to-cultivate-health-and-vitality-with-the-microcosmic-orbit/

Eger, E. (2020). *The gift: A survivor's journey to freedom.* Penguin Random House: UK.

Epstein, G. (2004). *Waking dream therapy: Unlocking the secrets of self through dreams and imagination.* ACMI Press: New York.

Feinstein, J., Buzza, C., Hurlemann, R., & Follmer, R.L. (2013). Fear and panic in humans with bilateral amygdala damage. *Nature Neuroscience, 16*(3), 270–272. DOI:10.1038/nn.3323.

Frankl, V.E. (1959). *Man's search for meaning.* Beacon Press: USA.

Hanh, T.N. (1991). *Peace is every step: The path of mindfulness in everyday life.* Bantam Books: New York.

Hanson, R., Shapiro, S., Hutton-Thamm, E., Hagerty, M.R., & Sullivan K.P. (2021). Learning to learn from positive experiences. *The Journal of Positive Psychology.* DOI:10.1080/17439760.2021.2006759

HeartMath Institute. Retrieved December 2022 from https://www.heartmath.org.

Hobson, J.A. (1994). *The chemistry of conscious states: How the brain changes its mind.* Little Brown & Co: Boston.

Jahnke, R. (2002). *The healing promise of qi: Creating extraordinary wellness through qigong and tai chi.* Contemporary Books: Chicago, IL.

Jahnke, R. (2022). Activate your inner healing elixirs with the 10 phases of qi cultivation. The shift network. Retrieved December 2022 from https://theshiftnetwork.com/course/43956/x

Kabbat-Zinn, J. (n.d.) *Guided mindfulness meditation practices with Jon Kabat-Zinn.* Retrieved December 2022 from https://www.mindfulnesscds.com

Kelley, H.M., Cunningham, T., & Branscome, J. (2015). Reflective journaling with at-risk students, *Vistas Online*, article 8. https://www.counseling.org/ knowledge-center/vistas/by-year2/vistas-2015/docs/default-source/vistas/ reflective-journaling-with-at-risk-students

Killingsworth, M.A. & Gilbert, D.T. (2010). A wandering mind is an unhappy mind, *Science*, *330*(6006), 932. DOI:10.1126/science.1192439

Koller, T. (2017). How visualization helped me overcome depression and how I've succeeded with mental illness. *Thrive Global*, 7 April. Retrieved December 2022 from https://medium.com/thrive-global/how-visualization-helped-me-overcome-depression-67a15676159f

Koschwanez, H.E., Kerse, N., Darragh, M., Jarrett, P., Booth, R.J., & Broadbent, E. (2013). Expressive writing and wound healing in older adults: A randomized controlled trial. *Psychosomatic Medicine*, *75*(6), 581–590. DOI:10.1097/ PSY.0b013e31829b7b2e

Lee, D. (2022). Radiant lotus women's qigong and the art of wuji hundun qigong. The shift network. Retrieved December 2022 from https://theshiftnetwork. com/course/01DLee08_22

Levine, P. (2010). In an unspoken voice: How the body releases trauma and restores goodness. North Atlantic Books: Berkeley, CA.

Lieberman, M.D., Eisenberger, N.I., Crockett, M.J., Tom, S.M., Pfeifer, J.H., & Way, B.M. (2007). Putting feelings into words: Affect labeling disrupts amygdala activity in response to affective stimuli. *Psychological Science*, *18*(5), 421–428. DOI:10.1111/j.1467-9280.2007.01916.x. PMID: 17576282.

Lin, S. (n.d.). *Laboratory for mind–body signaling & energy research*. Retrieved December 2022 from https://mindbodylab.bio.uci.edu

Loveday, P., Lovell, G., & Christian, J. (2016). The best possible selves intervention: A review of the literature to evaluate efficacy and guide future research. *Journal of Happiness Studies*, *19*(2), 607–628. DOI:10.1007/s10902-016-9824-z

Ma, X., Yue, Z.Q., Gong, Z.Q., Zhang, H., Duan, N.Y., Shi, Y.T., Wei, G.X., & Li, Y.F. (2017). The effect of diaphragmatic breathing on attention, negative affect and stress in healthy adults. *Frontiers in Psychology*, *8*, 874. https://doi. org/10.3389/fpsyg.2017.00874

McGlynn, F.D. (2002). Systematic desensitization. *Encyclopedia of psychotherapy*, M. Hersen & W. Sledge (eds). Academic Press: Cambridge, MA (pp. 755–764).

McKeown, P. *The oxygen advantage: The simple, scientifically proven breathing technique that will revolutionise your health and fitness*. Piatkus Books: London.

National Institute for the Clinical Application of Behavioral Medicine (NICABM). (n.d.). Expert ways to work with anxiety. Retrieved December 2022 from https://www.nicabm.com

National Institute for the Clinical Application of Behavioral Medicine (NICABM). (n.d.). How to work with the patterns that sustain depression. Retrieved December 2022 from https://www.nicabm.com.

Nattie, E. (1999). CO2, Brainstem chemoreceptors and breathing. *Progress in Neurobiology*, *59*(4), 299–331. DOI:10.1016/s0301-0082(99)00008-8

Naviaux, R.K. (2020). Perspective: Cell danger response biology – the new science that connects environmental health with mitochondria and the rising tide of chronic illness. *Mitochondrion, 51*, 40–45.

Neff, K. (n.d.) *Self-compassion with Dr. Kristin Neff*. Retrieved December 2022 from https://self-compassion.org

Nestor, J. (2020). *Breath: The new science of a lost art*. Penguin Life: UK.

Ogden, P., & Fisher, J. (2015). *Sensorimotor psychotherapy: Interventions for trauma and attachment*. W.W. Norton & Company: New York, London.

Olsson, A. (2014). *Conscious breathing: Discover the power of your breath*. Sorena: Stockholm, Sweden.

Podvoll, E. (2018). The history of sanity, *Windhorse Community Services*, 7 November. Retrieved December 2022 from https://windhorsecommunityservices.com/ journal-entry-018-the-history-of-sanity/

Porges, S.W. (2011). *The polyvagal theory: Neurophysiological foundations of emotions, attachment, communication, and self-regulation*. Norton Series on Interpersonal Neurobiology. W.W. Norton & Company: New York.

Rothenberg, R. (2019). *Restoring prana: A therapeutic guide to pranayama and healing through the breath for yoga therapists, yoga teachers and healthcare practitioners*. Jessica Kingsley Publishers: London.

Rozin, P., & Royzman, E. (2001). Negativity bias, negativity dominance, and contagion. *Personality and Social Psychology Review*, 5(4), 296–320.

Schwartz, A. (n.d.). *Arielle Schwartz, PhD, licensed clinical psychologist.* Retrieved December 2022 from https://drarielleschwartz.com

Shapiro, F. (2017). Eye movement desensitization and reprocessing (EMDR) therapy: Basic principles, protocols, and procedures, 3rd edn. The Guilford Press: New York.

Siegel, D.J. (2018). *Aware: The science and practice of presence.* TarcherPerigee: New York.

Smyth, J.M., Johnson, J.A., Auer, B.J., Lehman, E., Talamo, G., & Sciamanna, C.N. (2018). Online positive affect journaling in the improvement of mental distress and well-being in general medical patients with elevated anxiety symptoms: A preliminary randomized controlled trial. *Journal of Medical Internet Research: Mental Health*, 5(4), e11290. DOI:10.2196/11290. PMID: 30530460; PMCID: PMC6305886.

Stone, L. (2008). Just breathe: Building the case for email apnea. Huffington Post, 8 February. https://www.huffpost.com/entry/just-breathe-building-the_b_85651

Stone, L. (2014). Are you breathing? Do you have email apnea? *lindastone.net.* Retrieved December 2022 from https://lindastone.net/2014/11/24/are-you-breathing-do-you-have-email-apnea/

Tronick, E.Z. (1989). Emotions and emotional communication in infants. *American Psychologist*, 44(2), 112–119. https://doi.org/10.1037/0003-066X.44.2.112

Tronick, E. Z., & Gianino, A. (1986). Interactive mismatch and repair: Challenges to the coping infant. *Zero to Three*, 6(3), 1–6.

Velikova, S., Sjaaheim, H., & Nordtug, B. (2017). Can the psycho-emotional state be optimized by regular use of positive imagery?, Psychological and electroencephalographic study of self-guided training. *Frontiers in Human Neuroscience*, 10, 664. doi:10.3389/fnhum.2016.00664

Verges, S., Chacaroun, S., Godin-Ribuot, D., & Baillieul, S. (2015). Hypoxic conditioning as a new therapeutic modality. *Frontiers in Paediatrics*, 3, 58. https://doi.org/10.3389/fped.2015.00058

Walker, T.D. (2014). How Finland keeps kids focused through free play, *The Atlantic*, 30 June, https://www.theatlantic.com/education/archive/2014/06/how-finland-keeps-kids-focused/373544/

Walker, T.D. (2017). *Teach like Finland: 33 strategies for joyful classrooms.* W.W. Norton & Company: New York and London.

Weitzberg, E., & Lundberg, J. (2022). Humming greatly increases nasal nitric oxide. *American Journal of Respiratory and Critical Care Medicine*, *166*(2), 144–145. https://doi.org/10.1164/rccm.200202-138BC

Wolpe, J. (1958). *Psychotherapy by reciprocal inhibition.* Stanford University Press: Stanford, CA.

Finding mental health support

Wherever you are in the world, there are resources such as helplines, institutions and professionals that you can access for mental health support. Find out what is available in your area so you can reach out for support when you need it. Here are some helpful sites in different regions:

Australia

https://www.healthdirect.gov.au/mental-health-helplines

New Zealand

https://www.healthnavigator.org.nz/support/d/depression/

United Kingdom

https://www.mentalhealth.org.uk/explore-mental-health/get-help

United States of America

https://www.nimh.nih.gov/health/find-help

South Africa

https://www.sadag.org

Acknowledgements

A toolkit like this is the result of many years of learning, research, practice and support.

To start with I would not be able to invest my time and energy in a project like this without the loving support of my family. Thank you Stephen for your love and unwavering belief in me, as well as for your regular support on the business side of my creative endeavours. To our children, Emmah and Miela, thank you for being yourselves, for all the delight, laughter and energy you bring. Thank you also for being willing to learn and grow together as we navigate life's challenges.

A big, heartfelt thank you to Rockpool Publishing, led by Lisa Hanrahan and Paul Dennett. Without you, this book would not exist. I am eternally grateful for having found Rockpool and for my years of being a Rockpool author in the creation of meaningful, beautiful books that can make a difference in our world. Thank you to the whole team at Rockpool who worked on *Stress Less*. This includes Jessica Cox of Quick Fox Editing whose editing input honed the material to be as reader-friendly as possible and Daniel Poole for the magnificent design of the book from cover to cover.

Academically the foundation for my approach to psychology originates at Naropa University, where I graduated with a Masters degree in Somatic Psychology two decades ago. I remain grateful to all the teachers who inspired, enriched and educated me along the way. Special mention for this book is for Zoe Avstreih, Professor Emeritus at Naropa University, who wrote the foreword. Thank you Zoe for your wonderful words and generosity with your time and energy to read the book and write the foreword. I am deeply grateful. It is worth mentioning that it was in Zoe's classes two decades ago that I learned foundational skills for working with the realm of imagination and dreams that strongly influence how I work to this day. The 'Surprise me' visualisation exercise in this book is an adaptation of an exercise I learned from Zoe. Zoe also animated my understanding of living inside of my body through her classes in Authentic Movement that has also fundamentally influenced the way that I work as a Somatic Psychologist.

Over the last couple of decades, my professional experience and continued professional development have led me to accumulate and hone various skills for working with mental health in private practice and in the corporate sector. I have worked with individuals as a psychotherapist and coach and I have facilitated workshops and presented talks to groups on various topics, such as stress management, mindfulness and team or leadership development. Thank you to all my clients, from whom I learn just as much as they might learn from me. You all open my heart and mind regularly to our shared humanity and have provided me with plenty of opportunities to apply and refine my mind–body psychology tools for the promotion of mental health. It is through each of you that I have also learned to be creative and flexible as I regularly tailor my approach to best suit who I am working with. I have come to know well that what works for one person or organisation might not work for another, which is also why there is a variety of tools on offer in this book!

Another person to thank for an eye-opening introduction to the practice of acupressure and its applications for self-supportive touch is Dr Stephanie Mines. Dr Mines is the founder of The TARA Approach, a path for regenerative health informed by her experience as trauma expert, neuroscientist and embryologist. Dr Mines has always inspired me with her energy, passion, determination and drive to make a difference. Even though I do not work exactly by the Jin Shin TARA acupressure system that I was taught by Dr Mines back in 2002 and 2003, I do know through her about the immense value of learning to hold ourselves supportively. I also continue to draw creatively on self-supportive touch in this book as I have in previous ones.

For the research of this book I have many to thank, whose teachings and courses were greatly supportive at various stages. I would like to thank Ruth Buczynski, PhD, President and Licensed Psychologist at the National Institute for the Clinical Application of Behavioral Medicine (NICABM) for curating wonderfully informative and accessible online courses that I apply to my continued professional development. I have participated in courses on topics including anxiety and depression and have had the privilege to learn from thought leaders in the field of psychology such as Dr Kelly McGonigal, Dr Dan Siegel, Dr Rick Hanson, Dr Peter Levine, Dr Pat Ogden, Dr Ron Siegel, Dr Joan Borysenko, Dr Bessel van der Kolk, Dr Kristen Neff and Dr Christopher Germer, to name but a few. I also have appreciated over many years, drawing on the work of Dr Diane Poole Heller, creator of Trauma Solutions.

Another online platform for enriching courses that have supported both my research and personal growth, is The Shift Network. The Shift Network was founded by Stephen Dinan who is CEO of this network and a member of the Transformational Leadership Council and Evolutionary Leaders. My particular interest here has been studying the ancient art of qigong. Qigong draws on elements of mindful movement, breathing, visualisation and meditation with the intention of refining a sense of vitality, promoting well-being and serving as a foundation for martial arts practice. It is rooted in Chinese Medicine and Taoist philosophy and dates back thousands of years. The qigong grandmasters and world-renowned teachers that I have had the privilege to learn from through The Shift Network include Daisy Lee, Mantak Chia and Roger Jahnke. Particular mention is for Daisy Lee, with whom I have studied the most. Daisy, I so appreciate your gently powerful, inspiring and heartfelt presence. I bow to your many years of in-depth study with your qigong teachers, your dedication to spreading the timeless wisdom of qigong in general and your particular focus on raising awareness of qigong practices for women.

The movement practices created for this book are inspired by my evolving understanding of qigong that embeds mindful movement in the context of our innate connection with vital energy, nature and the greater universe.

Last, but not least, I would like to thank you, the reader, for investing your time and interest in reading this book. I hope that your life is richer for it.